Urban
REGENERATION

FRONT COVER:
Warehouses converted into housing at Atlantic Quay, Cardiff, South Wales.

BACK COVER:
The Cannery, San Francisco, one of the first 'festival markets' to be built in the USA.

REGEN

IAN COLQUHOUN

Urban

ERATION

An International Perspective

B.T. Batsford Ltd · London

© Ian Colquhoun 1995
First published 1995

Typeset by Latimer Trend & Company Ltd,
Plymouth
Printed in Singapore

for the publishers
B. T. Batsford Ltd
4 Fitzhardinge Street
London W1H 0AH

A CIP catalogue record for this book is
available from the British Library

ISBN 0 7134 7087 9

Contents

Acknowledgements

One of the major purposes of writing this book was to bring together and illustrate some of the best examples of urban regeneration that have been initiated in recent years. This would not have been possible without the generosity of the people who have helped to provide information, plans, drawings and other material. In a few instances, it has not been possible to trace the original source and it is hoped that no rights have been infringed. All photographs were taken by the author.

The vast majority of the information on the overseas projects came from the British Architectural Library at the RIBA, 66 Portland Place, London; the friendly help and advice from the librarians is an important aspect of a unique facility which is such a valuable resource to the architectural profession in Britain. Additional research was undertaken in the libraries of the University of Humberside and my thanks go to the staff there for their assistance. I am also indebted to Professor Brian Edwards of the University of Huddersfield, whose excellent book on the London Docklands was a great source of information.

A tour of urban regeneration projects in Scandinavia was made possible as a result of funding from the University of Humberside. Regrettably, it was only possible to refer briefly to the excellent projects in these countries. Thanks go to Ann Beer, Professor of Landscape Architecture at Sheffield University, for help with this visit.

My thanks go to Norman Reynolds for his graphics and to Richard Reynolds the Commissioning Editor, Martina Stansbie and the rest of the production team at B. T. Batsford for their patient help. I cannot thank my wife, Christine, enough. Her travel arrangements for visiting the projects and assistance with the photography were invaluable. She also prepared the index and the bibliography and generally did everything to allow me the time for the work. Thanks also to my daughter, Fiona, for accompanying me on some of the visits in Britain and for her research in Italy.

Where possible, acknowledgement has been given to the source of all references and the originators and/or architects of the plans and drawings. An additional reference is to *Offices into Flats* by James Barlow and David Gann (p. 23), which was published in 1993 by the Joseph Rowntree Foundation, York.

Further recognition is due for the following figures:

2: Plan reproduced by courtesy of Tyne and Wear Development Corporation who are the overall master plan coordinators. Several architects have been responsible for the individual projects. 7: Donald MacDonald of the Foyer Federation and the supervisor and staff of the Foyer de Jeunes Travailleurs, Avenue Charles V, Paris. 8: Luc Daveaux, Architect of the Foyer project in Orleans. 14: Bjorn Malbert of Chalmers Technology University, Gothenburg and Olle Lindkvist of Eriksbergs Forvaltinings AB, Gothenburg. 46, 47, 48 and 52: Developers, McCormac, Baron and Associates. 57: Fisher Friedman Associates, Architects. 66: Jari Virtanen and Peter Fredriksson, Union for Youth Housing in Finland, Helsinki. 69: Richard Temple-Cox, Chairman of the Castlevale Housing Action Trust and the Development of Planning and Architecture, Birmingham City Council. The architects involved in producing the Castlevale feasibility study were Mike Pritty, David Cauldwell, Nigel Davies and Tony Powell. 70: Chris Johnson, Chief Architect (housing) London Borough of Lewisham. 71: Waltham Forest Housing Action Trust. 73 and 76: Chris Purslow, Ian Duff, Kate Dougan, Jim Cooke, Ian McLeod and the library, Department of Architecture and Related Services, City of Glasgow District Council. 80: Based on Ordnance Survey map with the permission of the Controller of Her Majesty's Stationery Office © Crown Copyright. 81: Birmingham City Council. 86: Plan reproduced by courtesy of Cardiff Bay Development Corporation. 106: Plan reproduced by courtesy of London Docklands Development Corporation. 87: Rob Pearson and John Keyworth, Sheffield Development Corporation. 96: Plan reproduced by courtesy of Cardiff Bay Development Corporation. 106: Plan reproduced by courtesy of London Docklands Development Corporation. 107: Bill Stevenson, Bellway Homes (Urban Renewal Division); Andy Clark and Peter Wright, Planning Development Department, London Borough of Barking and Dagenham. 110, 111 and 113: Hans den Broeder, gemeente Rotterdam. 120, 124, 128 and 129: SPI, Berlin, Hartmut Brocke, Claus Meyer-Rogge, Dieter Ruhnke. 138, 140: Jonathan Rowley for research in Bologna and Bologna City Council. 141: Genoa City Council. 146 and 148: Reproduced by courtesy of Temple Bar Properties Limited, Dublin. 150: Focus Point, Dublin. 152, 153, 155, 157, 159, 160 and 163: L'Atelier Parisien d'Urbanism (APUR), Paris and Revue Paris-Projet, Paris.

Ian Colquhoun

July 1994

Introduction

Cities are under threat. They are in decline as people seek the alternative living of suburbia. Whilst the form of cities may change in the future, their survival as places in which to live and work – and as the economic, social and cultural focal point for a wider community – is vital to the survival of modern civilization. This means facing up to the dereliction and the poverty in the inner cities with determination and imagination. The issues place the skills of architects and planners at the centre of a vital debate.

This book endeavours to contribute to this debate by bringing together a wide variety of approaches to urban regeneration – the philosophies, the ideas, the principles and the examples – from Britain, the United States of America and a number of countries in Western Europe. It describes some of the means by which urban decline is being redressed in these countries, within their social, economic and political context. In some instances, the problems have demanded a multi-faceted approach and the background is too complex to offer more than a passing comment. The range of regeneration projects includes land reclamation, the revival of waterfront areas, the adaptive re-use of redundant buildings, new housing, the uplifting of residential neighbourhoods and estates, conservation, and many more. Most have a common theme which is the importance of creating diversity and variety in the built environment, and the provision of mixed uses where possible. The most successful projects have come from strong public leadership, both nationally and locally, and from the involvement of the local community in the decision making process.[1]

The all-important reason for looking at approaches in other countries is to learn from their experiences. Care must however be taken to avoid copying solutions out of context. The history of cities throughout the world is littered with many ideal solutions which went wrong because people – politicians as well as architects and planners – looked, with envy, at practices elsewhere without proper reference to their own cultural and social background. It is very easy, for example, to be lured towards the compelling ideal of the European model of the city with its concentrated, high-density core, but it has to be recognized that most Europeans prefer to live in suburbs just as people do in Britain and the USA. If cities are to compete with suburbia, they must offer a high quality of lifestyle opportunities; this is the challenge for all those involved in urban regeneration.

An important message in this book is that design, particularly urban design, is essential to the regeneration process. This is so frequently misunderstood or ignored. Good design in a city context requires a coherent sense of vision which relates to the particular place and circumstance: 'The architectural character of a city is a special kind of problem. Each city possesses an individual character. What seems beautiful and lovable in one city may be ugly and detestable in another . . . not just the materials but forms as well are bound up with the place, with the nature of the earth and of the air.'[2] In addition to making economic and commercial sense, the benefits of good design will affect everyone, and directly or indirectly influence the quality of their lives.

The book's first chapter considers the issues – the problems that most former industrialized cities are currently facing, the different approaches to the organization and management of urban regeneration, and design. The next three chapters look at current urban regeneration practice in the USA, Britain and Europe. Each chapter provides an overview and a description of a number of key projects in cities. The last chapter reflects upon the different approaches and picks out important changes in attitude and approach that are needed to ease the process of urban regeneration in most countries.

Fisherman's Wharf, San Francisco: the beginning of urban regeneration in the USA.

1 Issues, approaches and design

The issues

Economic and social background

It was the strong economic and social forces of the industrial revolution that created the large tracks of what is now termed 'the inner city', where factories were built and the workforce lived in densely packed housing. In the 1920s and 1930s, the motor car and the improvement of public transport enabled the more wealthy to move out to the suburbs. This began the drift away from the inner cities of skills and wealth which has continued to the present day. The significance of the forces that affected these areas in the 1960s and 1970s, is that the industrial and commercial base, upon which they had originally been founded, almost ceased to exist. The loss in the West of heavy industry and engineering to the Far Eastern and developing countries left vast areas of urban dereliction, vacant buildings, unemployment and poverty. This was accompanied by a substantial exodus of the remaining people and wealth to the suburbs and to the countryside beyond, leaving behind the poor and disadvantaged. Amongst these there are large concentrations of ethnic minorities.

The scene was familiar throughout the western world. From the 1970s more and more European countries began to report losses in their inner-city populations. In Britain the outward movement had already begun in the 1950s, following the government's massive slum clearance programme. Complete neighbourhoods of nineteenth-century houses were demolished and the areas rebuilt with large council estates. In order to house the

1 *Sensitive infill housing in Kreuzberg, Berlin.*

large numbers of people who were displaced by the clearance, new council housing was built on the outskirts of the city in what are known today as 'outer estates'. These now have their own problems which are not too dissimilar from those of the inner city. New Towns and planned overspill developments took even more people. The recession of the 1970s and 1980s hit the British economy and the inner cities with great force and over two million factory jobs were lost.

In the USA most cities have experienced an even greater outward migration of the population. Fuelled by cheaper land prices than in the inner city and the low cost of personal mobility, the new 'sub-cities' have grown extensively. With the people have gone the jobs and the decentralization of retailing into regional shopping malls. In her book *Death and Life of Great American Cities*, Jane Jacobs described the results of this as follows: 'The endless new developments spreading beyond the cities are reducing city and countryside alike to a monotonous, unnourishing gruel'.[1] Decentralization to the suburbs in the USA is now more rapid than at any time in history. 'We're moving everything: workplace, funplace, healthplace . . . the outcome is new suburban cities with one thing in common: they are growing in white, upper-middle-class areas'.[2]

Robert Reich, President Clinton's labour advisor, offered further comment when he remarked that cities have to recognize that they are in competition with each other for the limited resources to revive the economy of their inner-city areas. In some respect it can also be said that countries are in competition with each other. 'Those economies will succeed in the future which have the most up-to-date infrastructure and human skills to attract the fixed pool of mobile international investment' . . . but 'success comes from those areas improving their comparative advantage'.[3] Successful urban regeneration cannot,

therefore, be achieved in a vacuum. It requires cities to produce a comprehensive strategy based on local needs and opportunities. It also needs commitment and flexibility of approach to respond to new opportunities and changing circumstances as they arise.

It also requires the uneven economic growth between the inner city and the outer areas to be controlled by planning at metropolitan/regional level. John Landis has admirably analysed the possibilities in the USA in an article in *Built Environment*. He says that 'Precisely because central city populations have such a large stake in the growth of their regions (and because unmanaged growth has the potential for undermining the economy of the central city), it behoves city and suburban officials to consult and cooperate in planning the long-term growth of their regions, and to avoid the sorts of infrastructure development that will undermine existing public and private investments.'[4] Most western European countries already have some form of Regional government where these issues are considered but Britain and the USA have no such structure.

The pace of change is now so dramatic that, without intervention, the model of the city with which people have been familiar since the nineteenth century could rapidly become obsolete. Cities could ultimately revert back to their one-time role as centres of government, learning and culture, and sustain only the population size and physical extent necessary for those functions. Production would be almost exclusively based on non-material goods, information technology, advanced service sectors, etc., where the most common words will be new, light and flexible. The problem with this solution is what happens to the people who do not fit this model. This is the very essence of the urban regeneration issue.

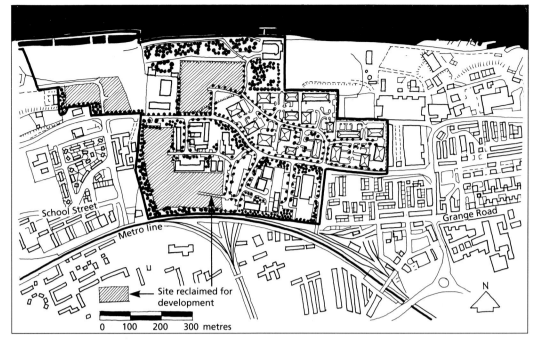

2 *Viking Industrial Park, Jarrow, Tyne and Wear.*

School Street

Metro line

Grange Road

N

Site reclaimed for development

0   100   200   300 metres

The need for cities: why it is so important to rejuvenate them

The great cities such as New York, London and Paris have always attracted a cosmopolitan upper and middle class population which is willing to pay to live near the heart of things.[5] A number of European cities have halted, or significantly slowed down, outward migration by building sensitive infill housing in their central areas (Fig. 1). There are lessons here, but inner cities have to be seen in the context that the impulse and the reason which drove people in Victorian times to build cities has gone. Conceptions of distance, journeys to work, transportation and communications have all changed completely in modern times, so that it is no longer necessary to live or conduct business in a city. If people are to be induced to invest their lives and hopes in the inner city, it is necessary to determine ways to make cities as a whole satisfy present day needs and aspirations; where this cannot be achieved, equally attractive alternatives must be developed.

Some people would argue that it is not necessary to spend large sums of money on urban regeneration: why not merely grass over the dereliction and let the cities decline. The response to this is complex. One reason for the importance of cities has already been given – the people who are already there are important. There is also

in existence the infrastructure to support the people. The second reason is that cities are and always will be the focal point of civilized life. In the words of Brian Robson, Professor of Geography at Manchester University, 'No cities, no civilization'.[6] The third reason is that cities came into being because people needed to transact business. Cities became market places to trade in money and commodities. Great cities dignified themselves with elegant buildings and fine spaces and this process continues today. Those nineteenth-century industrial cities which have striven to create a strong image of themselves in recent years are now finding the investment of great benefit to their economic recovery.

There are however more simple reasons why cities are necessary. The experience of suburbia on a huge scale in the USA is sufficient to see that the alternative has serious problems. Principal amongst these are that thinly spread, suburban development cannot support good public transport, neighbourhood shopping or local industry, nor generate lively communities. Also the thinner, dispersed city has proved to be ecologically unsound. It relies heavily on the car, creating unmanageable levels of congestion and pollution, and it eats up valuable green spaces. In this connection Jane Jacobs referred to the need for cities as follows. 'For centuries, probably everyone who has thought about cities at all has noticed that

there seems to be some connection between the concentration of people and the specialities they can support.'[7] She also refers to the conclusions of John H. Denton, professor of business at the University of Arizona, who, after studying American suburbs and British New Towns came to the conclusion that 'such places must rely on ready access to a city for protection of their cultural opportunities … decentralization produced such a thin population spread that the only effective economic demand that could exist in suburbs was that of the majority. The only goods and cultural activities available will be those that the majority requires'.[8]

This opinion is supported by Richard Rogers and Mark Fisher in their book *A New London*. In answering their own question 'why are cities important?', they comment that 'urban density provides the best setting for the easy, face-to-face interaction and communication that generates the scientific, technological and cultural creativity that is the engine of economic prosperity in the post-industrial age. Economists and urban planners who

once thought that telecommunications would render redundant the dense city, with its downtown financial district, now know otherwise'.[9]

Poverty and unemployment in the inner city

Cities have always been repositories for the poor, but today's poor are different from the migrants and immigrants of the past who worked their way up from a pick and shovel or a sewing machine. There are two major reasons: the first has to do with a permanent change in the western economy and the second with the increasingly rapid suburbanization already mentioned. As the economy has changed from the manufacture and distribution of material goods to service and knowledge-based industries, vast numbers of blue collar jobs have disappeared. This, added to the loss of middle-income urban manufacturing jobs, has created a city labour market that is polarized between highly paid professional work and badly paid service jobs. There is little place for the person in between. The flight from the

3 *Newcastle business park built on the site of a former armoury works on the banks of the River Tyne.*

inner city has not only left behind the wastelands but people with the least education who are least able to cope.

Some groups of people have been hit particularly hard, especially those who face other difficulties with their lives. Those who suffer ill health or disability, and younger and older workers, single parent families, the ethnic minorities, are all particularly vulnerable to unemployment. For the older worker made redundant, the loss of the job has meant premature, enforced retirement and loss of personal dignity. Poverty is not however only about shortage of money. *Faith in the City*, the report of the Archbishop of Canterbury's commission on Urban Priority Areas in Britain, published in 1985, advised that 'it is about rights and relationships; about how people are treated and how they regard themselves; about powerlessness, exclusion, and loss of dignity. Yet the lack of an adequate income is at its heart'.[10] There has been a case made that the benefits of economic growth will 'trickle down' to unemployed people in the inner cities, but there is little evidence to date to prove this theory.

Since the early 1980s, the increasingly competitive pressures in international markets requires firms to modernize to stay in competition. The result will be different and fewer jobs. For cities to remain competitive it is vital for them to attract the new high technology industries. However, encouraging these into the inner city is not easy. Their preferred location is the out-of-town, highly landscaped, business park (with its modern factories), room for expansion at low cost, a pleasant environment, good infrastructure and proximity to the major highway network.

People in cities are trying to respond by developing their own business parks (Figs. 2 and 3), but experience to date indicates that this 'macro' economic approach may only have a marginal effect on unemployment levels in the inner city. The reality is that, without a change of philosophy away from a total reliance on the market economy, unemployment is likely to remain permanently at a high level in the inner city. The challenge that government at national and local levels in all countries in the western world now have to face is how can people, who are unable to find employment, be offered an opportunity to carry out work which the community will value, and from which they gain their own self-respect and self-esteem. This could mean evolving a new concept for work as a whole.

One approach could be to foster small, local, 'micro'-scale enterprise. An example is described later in the paragraphs on Bologna. This approach has the benefit of being able to be physically accommodated within the inner city fabric, close to where the people live. Such solutions, however, require public support to survive in the early years, but they would be a sounder investment than spending huge sums to subsidize unemployment.

Housing

The most obvious feature of the inner city is its physical dilapidation as measured by housing conditions. Housing is becoming increasingly polarized between inner and outer areas; poor people are trapped in inadequate housing in the inner cities whilst the more affluent and young families choose the suburbs. Poverty in housing is aggravated by the frequent unsuitability of the design and layout to cope with the pressures of modern-day society, which can be more acute in the inner cities than elsewhere.

Unemployment, the breakdown of family relationships, the increase in single parent families, the increasing desire on the part of young people to establish their own home, concentrations of ethnic and minority groups, etc., all produce extra strains in the inner cities. The scene in the United States is summed up by Andrea Dean who in 1988 wrote in *Architecture*, the Journal of the American Institute of

Architects, that 'the 1949 housing bill promised a decent home and a suitable environment for every American family. Forty years later the most sordid slums look good to millions of Americans who have no homes at all. Our housing situation is the nation's shame and the prospects for turning it round look fairly grim'.[11] Brian Robson, Professor of Geography at Manchester University, has described the problems in Britain in terms of the 'nightmare scenario in which inner cities become ghettos of the poor, guarded by armed police, while better-off areas a couple of bus stops away hire their own armed guards'.

Governments in both Britain and the USA have failed to see the link between urban renewal and housing. Urban renewal on the scale required will never take place unless there is sufficient public investment in refurbishing the existing stock of housing, and the supply of new rented housing is also increased. This also needs a comprehensive housing subsidy strategy which deals fairly with all tenures, enabling all households to have a choice of adequate and affordable housing.

In Western Europe a great deal more imagination and insight has been shown. Some countries have demonstrated that it is possible to evolve large-scale social housing programmes to cope with the ever rising needs; and that these can 'have relevance to the particularities of place and custom'[12] (Fig. 4). It is only necessary to look to some of the large inner-city estates built between the wars in Amsterdam, Berlin and Vienna to prove this point (Fig. 5). Peter Davy comments in *The Architectural Review* that 'It is perhaps rather more difficult for Anglo-Saxon cultures, where the traditional perception of dwelling has been the house, rather than the flat, to generate quite such a convincing relationship between traditional morphology and the present need to build contemporary housing on a large scale. Yet it is not impossible . . . there is a

4 *New housing in the mixed-use development at Aker Brygge, Oslo.*

distinguished succession of American condominium developments that stretches far back . . . which suggest that workable low-rise, high-density geometries could be evolved for housing schemes for the less rich that combine a respect for the individual dwelling with a sense of place and community' (Fig. 6).[13]

Homelessness

Most large cities have their share of people sleeping on the streets, and the 'homeless and hungry' signs of beggars at underground stations and other well-peopled locations. 'Such conditions permeate all aspects of the life of a city and can threaten its economic viability'.[14] Traditionally, the public perception of the homeless was an alcoholic, elderly man or a mentally disturbed, middle-aged woman, but during the 1980s the picture changed dramatically. A new, more vulnerable group was emerging as both young people and families were finding themselves without a home and on the street. Homelessness has reached high proportions in the USA, with upwards of three million people without a place to live. As with poverty, homelessness is afflicting the young most viciously, and of the number of people who are homeless in the USA, half a million are children.[15] There are no accurate statistics on homeless people in the countries of mainland Europe and in particular of young homeless people, but the estimate is

5 *The refurbished Karl-Marx-Hof, Vienna, built in the 1920s, continues to provide good inner-city housing.*

6 *New urban housing, Pittsburgh.*

that there are between a million and a million and a half.[16] In Britain the rise in homelessness coincided with severe cut-backs in public funding for social housing. The total number of households accepted as homeless in 1992 was 141,860,[17] but the real figure of people in need is likely to be much more. The French have adopted the most advanced programme of action for young, homeless people with the development of 'Foyer' housing in most of their inner cities. These combine the opportunity of a home in pleasant buildings containing restaurants, recreation rooms, workshops and classrooms (Figs. 7 and 8). The young people learn life and employment skills as a condition of being offered accommodation.[18] The Dutch have similar schemes (p. 114) whilst in Germany the emphasis is on self-help (p. 127). Housing designed specially for young people has been built in Britain for many years (Fig. 9), but the small number has failed to meet the problems of homelessness in most large cities. There is now considerable interest in the Foyer concept which has its value, though the main requirement is for ordinary housing built into existing communities. There are also a number of very successful self-help projects that have been developed in recent years (p. 94).

Education

There is not the slightest doubt that most inner-city children are at a disadvantage from the moment they are born. Criticism is often directed at inner-city schools with little understanding of the difficulties which the teachers face, particularly in areas with large ethnic populations where several languages are spoken. Children are trapped in the inner city because they attend schools which – despite extra resources in some cases – are too full of other children with the same deprived backgrounds as themselves. Furthermore, contemporary youth culture is intensely hostile to the education system and in the

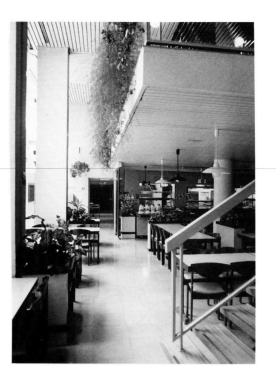

background of the inner city there is little incentive to change. The school system therefore turns out teenagers without the qualifications or the willpower to compete for jobs. The result is the prospect of unemployment for life. The solution in Britain has been to build new City Technology Colleges in inner-city areas. These are 'secondary schools in urban areas offering free education with a strong element of science and technology'. The government has always intended that the City Technology Colleges would be partially funded by the private sector. However, to date few companies have made a significant financial contribution.[19] The schools/industry compact follows the American model whereby partnerships are established between schools and local businesses. Neither of these initiatives are having real impact and what is required are smaller classes (with ability to cope with specialist needs), better and more regularly maintained buildings, and a vast expansion of nursery education which is more common in other countries in Western Europe (Fig. 10).[19]

7 *'Foyer Housing' in the centre of Paris offers excellent housing to young homeless people.*

Health

It is a well-known fact that people who live in deprived areas are less healthy and less well provided for than people who live in more prosperous areas. In her report 'The Health Divide: inequalities in health in the 1980s' Margaret Whitehead wrote that in Britain 'The unemployed and their families have considerably worse physical and mental health than those in work'.[20] She also observed that the multi-ethnic character of many inner-city areas added a further dimension to the issue. In these circumstances it is vital that community-based health initiatives are developed as much as possible. Most important of all, attention needs to be given to the social, economic, housing, environmental and emotional factors which contribute to ill health. *Faith in the City* summed this up in the few following words – 'Underlying

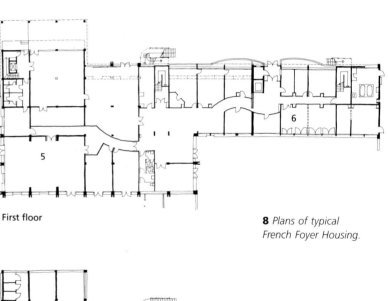

First floor

8 *Plans of typical French Foyer Housing.*

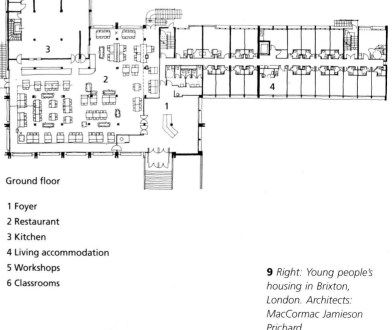

Ground floor

1 Foyer
2 Restaurant
3 Kitchen
4 Living accommodation
5 Workshops
6 Classrooms

9 *Right: Young people's housing in Brixton, London. Architects: MacCormac Jamieson Prichard.*

the problem of disease is the more fundamental problem of unease which has its roots in factors such as anxiety, low personal esteem, broken relationships, and the stress of poverty, deprivation, unemployment and bad housing'.[21]

Law and order

Urban crime in the inner city is not a new phenomenon but it is increasing as urban deprivation increases. However, Jane Jacobs wrote that 'the thinning out of a city does not insure safety from crime and fear of crime'.[22] She advised that city streets that are well-populated and have good street lighting present fewer risks than the suburbs. Lord Scarman, when advising the British Government of the causes of the 1981 riots in London's Brixton, considered that unemployment was a major factor that increased crime in urban areas.[23] *Faith in the City* commented that 'Vandalism may often be a protest against the inhumanity of the environment and an attempt to soften some of its harshness . . . our experience suggests that where a community is constructed on a scale small enough for human relations to be conducted, and for the environment to be cared for by people who live within it, the destructiveness diminishes'.[24]

Transport

Nowhere is the impact of urban highways on inner-city areas more prominent than it is in the large cities of the USA. In many American cities, highway development has proved to be one of the most contentious issues in neighbourhood politics and a powerful force in mobilizing communities which might otherwise be politically inert (p. 41). In some instances, resident groups have been successful in securing the removal of raised highway, e.g. along the San Francisco waterfront (p. 61).[25] This is in sharp contrast to Britain, where proposed new highways are still a threat to inner cities. The engineered lines of these roads rarely relate to the urban grain of the city. Traffic planners in Britain should

learn from the experience in Barcelona where one of the major roads of Europe passes through the heart of the Olympic Village. The design of the road has been thought of sensitively in townscape terms for it either fits into the grid pattern of city streets as a planted boulevard or it is built into a cutting.

Most major cities in Western Europe and the USA have convenient rapid transit, underground, tramway, or bus systems (Fig. 11). Many are extending these to meet increasing need. a number have commissioned well-known architects to design the new buildings, e.g. Genoa (p. 141). Britain has started to catch up with a series of new developments such as the Tyne and Wear Metro, and the new tramways in Manchester and Sheffield, but progress is slow. The deregulation of public transport, by which cities have insufficient control over the routing and frequency of services, seems to bear little relationship to the policy of investing in new transit systems.

The lack of planning in London has meant that the average vehicle speed in the centre of the city has fallen to as low as 10 m.p.h., which is little faster than the horse and cart at the turn of the century.[26] The London Underground is painfully

10 *Kindergarten in Charlottenburg, Berlin.*

overcrowded (a 29 per cent increase in use over the period 1980 to 1990) whilst the number of bus passengers has declined.[27] It took a long time to gain government approval for the promised extension to the Jubilee underground line, despite its importance to urban regeneration in the London Docklands.

The poorer people who live in the inner city might appear to have a geographical advantage, but in reality they are still the most disadvantaged, particularly women. They are more likely to work part-time, and their average earnings are lower than those of men. Black and ethnic minority women are frequently in the lowest-paid jobs. Women form the majority of disabled people and elderly, especially in inner London. With age comes a loss of income and an increasing dependence for many people on public transport. To improve the situation is not impossible. It requires investment to build and operate the system, but cities in Europe and the USA have shown that this is possible even in difficult economic circumstances. In 1989, London's public transport fares were subsidized to the tune of 22 per cent, compared with Rotterdam's 83 per cent, Frankfurt's 55 per cent and Rome's 76 per cent. These levels of subsidy have changed little since 1989.[28]

11 *Rapid transport system in Pittsburgh.*

Dispersal of retailing

Despite the new surge of downtown retail development, most large departmental shops in the USA have moved to the suburbs, except in the case of the very large cities such as New York. Unfortunately this trend is becoming common in Britain and elsewhere in Europe. The large, air-conditioned mall is proving highly popular. However, in Europe shopping is still an urban function but the competition from the new out-of-town centres is fast gaining ground. To keep hold of the trade, city authorities are having to change the image of the central areas by improving the pedestrian environment, developing their own malls and covered shopping streets, and exploiting their leisure and tourist attractions. For the inner-city poor, these initiatives are vital as the car-based shopping mall is frequently inaccessible by public transport. Furthermore, the large supermarkets are killing off local traders who can only survive by charging more for their goods. Therefore, not only are people in the inner city the poorest in society, but they may have to pay more for their basic requirements.

Re-use of old buildings

The 're-cycling' of mills and warehouses is well established in the USA. The Americans have been particularly successful in converting buildings into places where people can buy unusual and specialist products – 'festival markets'. Baltimore's waterfront and Boston's Quincy Market are perhaps the best known (pp. 36 and 39). Covent Garden in London was one of the first similar developments in Britain. To carry out the developments, the Americans developed the concept of mixed public/private funding with the public monies acting as a lever for subsequent private sector investment.

In the United States, it has been proven that there is virtually no limit to the uses

for old buildings in the right location (Fig. 12). They offer distinctive places in which to live and in inner-city locations they have been very popular with young people and business people. Some of the best examples in Europe are in London Docklands (p. 108), Amsterdam (p. 125) and Hamburg (p. 136). Other uses include workspace for small firms, community workshops where people can learn a skill, innovation centres with links to higher education, enterprise centres and various kinds of business centres, all of which are essentially serviced office suites or miniature industrial estates within one complex of buildings. Recreational and leisure uses are common, including art galleries and sports centres which require large areas of cheap, flexible space; also hotels and community centres.

In Britain, public funding for the conservation of old buildings can come from a variety of sources. It can be funded from City Challenge as part of a wider area strategy. English Heritage make grants available, but these are limited. In a number of cities, Buildings Preservation Trusts have been established. The Bristol Trust, for example, has been one of the most successful in renovating over three quarters of the derelict buildings in the city centre since it was set up in 1982. Each Trust is a private limited company which is self-financing by way of a 'revolving fund'. The Trust purchases, restores, and sells historic buildings following their conversion to new uses. The Architectural Heritage Fund, established in 1976, offers loans to new trusts to enable them to become established and to acquire their first buildings to restore.[29] In the USA, the Pittsburgh History and Landmarks Foundation (p. 49), and similar organizations in other cities, operate almost identical schemes (p. 88).

Another way to re-use old buildings in inner-city areas is to convert redundant spaces above shops for housing. The

publication *Living over the Shop*,[30] which was written by Ann Petherick and Ross Fraser in 1992 of the University of York, offers good guidance on the principles and procedures. Unfortunately, whilst there have been some excellent schemes, e.g. 9 Berwick Street, London (where the upper floors were converted by the Soho Housing Association into one bedroom flats and a bedsit unit), the take-up of the funding made available by the government has been low.

The possibility of using empty office space for residential accommodation has also been recently explored. In their report *Offices into Flats*, James Barlow and David Gann advise that certain types of office building can be suitable. The main factor affecting conversion potential is the penetration of natural light into the interiors. The major problem is convincing the owners to accept a lower return for their investment.

Leisure and culture

People who live in inner-city areas tend to be low participants in sport and recreation, yet the benefits in terms of better health, personal development and achievement are immense. The potential for the sport and leisure industry to be a catalyst for inner-city jobs and economic regeneration are considerable. The importance of sport and recreation as tools in achieving a number of other objectives is now widely recognized. For example, the police and the probation service in Britain and the USA both recognize sport's potential to provide satisfying and demanding activities through which young people can learn to accept a level of authority and achieve personal success for perhaps the first time.

A number of cities such as Barcelona, Pittsburgh and Sheffield have developed large sports, leisure and cultural complexes as part of their strategy for improving the quality of life (Fig. 13). In reality, many of these facilities are used by the car-owning, better-off members of society, rather than

12 *Union Station, Washington DC, which has been superbly refurbished by Benjamin Thompson Associates.*

by people living locally. This is almost certainly the case with the buildings built in Barcelona for the 1992 Olympic Games, which are fenced and locked for much of the day; also several of the new facilities in Sheffield are underused or are too expensive for many people to use. An alternative, or complementary, strategy is to enable communities to develop and run their own provision. Buildings can be converted by them to provide a mixture of sport and community activities ranging from football to badminton, bowls, and other indoor pursuits for elderly people and play schemes for the young. The Department of the Environment's 'Sport and Recreation Provision in the Inner City', in advising of good practice in Britain, recommends the greater use of facilities in schools out of hours. It recognizes that there are problems with dual use but advises that 'It behoves every education authority, school governing body and head teacher to consider seriously the options for dual use of their facilities, facilities which the local community has paid for'.[31]

The location of open spaces, parks and children's play areas in the inner city are vital – even the smallest piece of land in the inner city can provide the opportunity for play. Experience in the Netherlands and Germany suggests that if proper thought and care is given to the design of these spaces, they can add considerably to the quality of a neighbourhood as a whole, without the children being a nuisance.[32]

The relationship between cultural development and urban regeneration is still not fully recognized in Britain at government level. Spending money on the arts and promoting it as part of a city's economic regeneration has, for many years, been seen by most major cities in Europe and the USA as a means of attracting inward investment. For those cities in Britain, e.g. Birmingham, Glasgow and Leeds, which seek 'European' or 'international' status as a significant part of

their economic regeneration strategy, the provision of theatres, concert halls, art galleries and museums is important to their programme of development.[33]

Land values and ownership

It is not uncommon for derelict land in inner-city areas to stand empty whilst its owner awaits its most financially beneficial use. Planning can assist in determining ways in which land can be used but there is no substitute for the land belonging to the organization that is to be responsible for its development. This may mean compulsory acquisition but this should be at a value that takes account of its preferred use in planning terms. This could be met by the landowner being bound to invest part of the profits in providing infrastructure works as a partner in the urban regeneration process – a measure that could help particularly where land is polluted. It could also mean that increases in value during implementation could be retained, in part at least, for the benefit of the existing and/or new community. Land values and ownership have been subject to intense political debate in most countries. Somehow a balance needs to be achieved if the issues are not to prohibit the effective use of land in the inner cities.

Green issues

Green issues are not only about the provision of open space and planting. They are concerned with developing cities which are 'ecological' and 'sustainable'. In addition to the quality of the natural environment, a number of other issues – energy, transport, waste and pollution – are all now re-occurring topics of concern when discussing the future of cities. The

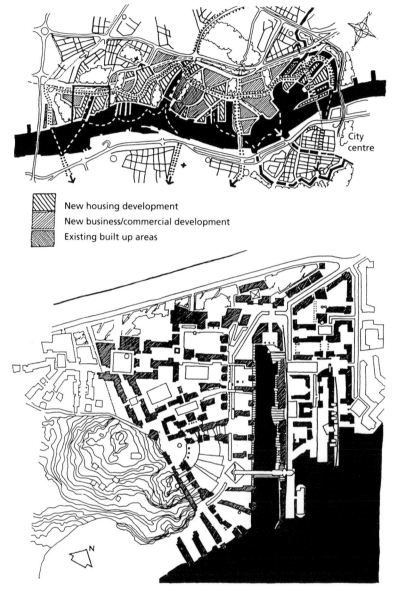

New housing development
New business/commercial development
Existing built up areas

14 *Urban design is an important part of the regeneration process. The drawings illustrate dockland regeneration in Gothenburg, Sweden. Top: concept plan by Ralph Erskine and others. Bottom: competition winning design for a site at Eriksberg by Danish architects, Arkos Arkitekter.*

debate is about producing development patterns that minimize the need for travel, increase the potential for public transport, permit higher densities at centres, discouraging the 'out-of-town' developments. These topics impinge directly on the viability of cities in the future. The inner cities may be too far gone in a downward spiral by the time they have been determined.

Approaches to the organization of urban regeneration

There are a number of different approaches to the organization of urban regeneration which relate to political outlook. Professor Ray Pahl has suggested seven as follows:[34]

1 That which perceives the problem in terms of the efficiency of service delivery by government agencies and free enterprise. Solutions are seen to depend on increasing the efficiency of bureaucracy and free enterprise by the use of managerial expertise.

2 That of the self-help anarchist who is also concerned with services, but argues that they should be locally rather than centrally administered. The quality of the service in terms of the recipients is seen as more important than the actual goods delivered. It is also argued by some that centralized systems are in any case incapable of delivering services to a diversified market. The solution is to encourage small-scale self-build projects.

3 The Marxist approach which insists that there can be no solution until government gains control over the free flows of capital in the private sector. Solutions depend on the political mobilization of the working classes.

4 The approach of the pragmatists and realists who consider that a timid piecemeal solution is inevitable, and who are primarily concerned to work out precisely what is and what is not feasible within the existing political framework. Some people in this camp even insist that the problem is not political at all.

5 The view put forward mainly by people working on the ground that the solution lies in encouraging local grass-roots activity, because existing central and local government are incapable of, and/or uninterested in, coping with the needs of the poor and the deprived. The most important thing is the desire of local people to control their own lives and work, and the need for them to 'discover their own humanity'. Policies should aim to achieve people's aspirations rather than the other way round.

6 The view of those who reject the bureaucratic encumbrances of government controls, and believe in the encouragement of small scale free enterprise activities, both community and capitalist inspired.

7 The view of the 'one-off fixers', who want to put in consultants, decide on priorities, timing and a budget, and then send a task force in to do the job.

These approaches are incompatible with each other, but all are individually appropriate to certain situations. Some have leanings in particular political directions. The key is to choose the best available means to suit the circumstance.

In practice the organization of urban regeneration requires the combination of a number of ingredients which are as follows:

1 There must be a catalyst – someone to trigger off the urban regeneration initiative.

2 Someone has to have vision to know where the regeneration effort is going.

Before anyone will put money into an area, an assessment of the economic potential has to be made. There is clearly an important planning and architectural input required at this stage. But if the proposals are not well thought through, they can quickly create disillusionment, because they are impracticable, non-fundable or just impossible.

3 There has to be a strategy but with no more than two or three main planks. The importance of the strategy is that the direction needs to be clearly pointed. The initiative has to capture the vision referred to above, holding on to the flagship projects and ideas. It should not attempt to cope with everything.

4 There has to be a proper legal and financial framework which ensures that there are formal links to the city, the developers and the planning authorities. All parties must be allowed to play their own particular role in the process. This may mean accepting that the private developer is best able to perceive market trends. To avoid conflict between this and community requirements, everyone involved should set out their objectives for the project right from the beginning. This enables all of the costs to be accommodated at the feasibility stage and, if necessary, written into the legal and financial framework. Thereafter, change of mind should be avoided.

5 Sensitivity of approach which requires time and effort. This calls for an understanding of the wider issues in the area and the hopes and aspirations of the people on the ground. Also, the political framework, both nationally and locally, needs to be fully understood.

6 It is most important to involve the local community. The policy should be to enhance the status of the inner city area, recognizing its local values and giving the

15 *The new urban park at Coin Street, London, was provided as a result of pressure from the local residents.*

16 *Conservation was an important part of the urban regeneration process in Boston, MA. USA.*

people who live, work and invest there a greater commitment to its future. The aim should be to raise the people's living standards, widen their choice, improve environmental, housing and economic conditions. The people policy should talk about the quality of life in the inner area and the life chances of its residents. It should face up to the concentration of poverty and relative depravation in the inner city rather than simply achieving the renewal of the physical environment to satisfactory standards. The policy must go beyond concern with urban renewal or economic regeneration, into issues raised by poverty and relative deprivation.[35]

Paul Davies, Head of the Civic Trust's Urban Regeneration Unit set up by the Civic Trust to advise on urban regeneration throughout Britain, emphasized in an interview in *The Planner* (4 September 1992) that 'Urban regeneration must be grass roots up, not imposed top down. It must be purpose-designed to meet particular local circumstances and needs, not done to a standard, centralized formula. People, places and business equal prosperity . . . economic, social and environmental benefits all interact. Regeneration only works really well if it has firm local roots. A locally based project and intensive local action is crucial to the effectiveness and suitability of regeneration, especially in view of centralist tendencies in both Whitehall and town hall.'[36]

Davies also warns against the propensity of politicians and others to expect too quick results. This is very much the case in Britain as Urban Development Corporations, Housing Action Trusts, etc. have only a very short life-span. Davies considers that three to four years is not long enough for any organization to become effective and that ten years is a more realistic time for showing genuine and lasting results in urban regeneration.

Design

Urban design

The overriding requirement for an effective approach to urban regeneration is that the professionals involved should possess a sense of vision, both in the management of the projects and the design. For architects and planners this means developing three-dimensional urban design skills and an ability to think about spacial issues on a large scale (Fig. 14). Richard MacCormac, President of the Royal Institute of British Architects, summed up the importance of urban design to urban regeneration when in 1993 he wrote that 'Urban design is part of a visionary building process, a focus for community action, and an affirmation of confidence in the potential of a place which is attractive to business investment'.[37]

However, it is regrettable that in Britain design quality all too often comes at the bottom of the priorities of developers and financiers. Yet, the more economically depressed an area is, the more it needs a quality approach to regeneration. There is sound guidance on the issues in *Inner City Regeneration and Good Design*, written for the Royal Fine Arts Commission in 1988 by Tony Aldous. Its principal recommendations are:[38]

1 In relation to buildings, landscape and public places, a sound mechanism for maintenance is crucial to preserve both amenity and investment.

2 There should be a mechanism to allow public bodies selling land to take a smaller initial payment and an equity in the development's future performance. This would address the all-too-frequent problem that 'the requirement to obtain the highest price militates against quality; and frustration among some of the better developers that, when they respond to design requirements, they are beaten on price by others who do not. This would put a premium on quality – and durable value – instead of what is often a penalty'.

3 Shotgun marriages between architects and developers are a recipe for disaster. Developer/architect competitions should be encouraged where these are viable. Good architects need to seek out up-and-coming developers and actively sell their skills.

4 There should be a considerable diversity in architectural approach, but within a strong urban design framework. The Bologna arcades (p. 141) were considered the kind of element which gives unity yet allows diversity of materials and form.

5 Landscape should be a key ingredient in the early preparation of a design framework for a development. Structure planting can be the 'glue' that 'holds the cityscape or landscape together'[39] (Fig. 15).

6 Defensible space should be high on any design check list. It is no use producing a good-looking building or landscape if it has pockets of indefensible space which are an invitation to crime and vandalism.

7 Effective mechanisms to maintain well-designed buildings and environments are a good investment, but are too-seldom adopted. In landscape at least, this is best achieved by including provision for the first five years' maintenance in the capital budget.

8 Very basic design guidance is needed for the small builder-developers, e.g. those who build small factories and workshops, do not use architects and are unlikely ever to do so. A modern equivalent of Georgian pattern books might produce an improvement in streetscape/townscape. This would enable them to build decently in an appropriate material to an appropriate pattern.

9 Conservation should be regarded as an integral part of the planning process, on a par with, for instance, density – not as 'the cream on the top'. Developers and planning authorities should be more aware of the possibilities for the re-use of buildings, their value as established elements in the townscape, and their potential once refurbished for enhancing the appearance of regeneration areas (Fig. 16). For all but the most special buildings, there must be flexibility and compromise to allow beneficial adaptation. Provided the spirit of a building or place is maintained, 'recycling' can be accepted as an alternative to restoration.

10 Continuing public involvement is the prerequisite for good appearance and amenity, especially in housing. Poor communication is a recipe for disaster in urban regeneration projects. Promoters and designers can be too busy putting together a package that they think will work, and forget the importance of communicating their intentions effectively to those – including local government and local communities – who are in a position to either support or oppose and block them. The design of the scheme is at least as open to misunderstanding as any other element. Developers' and designers' intentions for urban regeneration need to be 'marketed' to the community and local leaders.

11 A 'highest upfront price' requirement leads to developers over-bidding and then cutting on quality. Walter Sondheim, Chairman of the Baltimore Development Agency, advises on price bidding as follows:

* Upfront-payment-plus-equity is a reasonable basis for ensuring that the public exchequer gets a proper return.

* This makes for better quality and therefore a more durable investment.

* Over the years the actual return to the exchequer is likely to be greater than in the case of a purely upfront formula.

This expert advice is admirable but there is no substitute for the involvement of competent urban designers with both the vision to see the three-dimensional solutions and the ability to communicate these. This requires skills beyond those of normal architectural and planning practice which can only come from design maturity and practice.

Design workshops

An effective means of developing ideas quickly are design workshops. These can bring together the developers, the city council officials and the local people to work with the professionals. In the USA these have taken the form of Regional/Urban Design Assistance Teams (R/UDAT). These are organized by the American Institute of Architects. The German equivalent is the 'Bauforum' (p. 136). In Britain workshops have been particularly useful in stimulating ideas from the local people and giving them a sense of involvement. Richard MacCormac, while he was RIBA President between 1991 and 1993, organized 18 workshops throughout the country which indicated 'how rapidly and effectively urban design can create new perceptions in situations which have resisted the conventional processes of business and local government'. Workshops can be more useful than design competitions, although these have their place in the right circumstance, as the presence of so many people working together and exchanging ideas can be more stimulating than people working alone in a vacuum.

17 The Inner Harbor, Baltimore.

2 The American example

The major approaches to urban regeneration in the USA

There are two main strands to the urban regeneration in American cities: the revitalization of the downtown areas, and neighbourhood renewal and housing. Although city authorities give most publicity to their revitalized central areas, housing activity is significant. In fact it could be argued that the real urban regeneration lesson to come from American cities is not from the partnership of government and business or from the fine waterfront developments that this has produced, but from the action of residents of local communities in the inner urban areas, often against great opposition (Fig. 18).[1]

The revitalization of downtown areas

The most striking downtown developments are those which have resulted from the rejuvenation of the former decaying waterfront areas in the cities that were formerly the great ports of the USA (Fig. 17). These areas had progressively declined from the 1950s due to the migration of shipping downstream to deep water where it was possible to locate bulk terminals, container ports and roll-on/roll-off methods of loading and unloading ships. It also arose from the emergence of large shipping organizations and the loss of smaller locally-based companies. The first 'festival market' was built in San Francisco in the 1950s; the idea gained international recognition in the 1970s and 1980s from Baltimore's Inner Harbor and Boston's Quincy Market and waterfront schemes.

The funding came from a mixture of public and private sources. Government legislation in 1977 introduced the Urban Development Action Grant (UDAG) with the intention that there should be a public/private ratio of investment into urban regeneration projects of between 1 to 4.5 and 1 to 6.5.[1] The process is well documented in Professor Peter Hall's book, *Cities of Tomorrow*. He writes that:

> The magic recipe for urban revitalization . . . seemed to consist of a new kind of creative partnership . . . between the city government and the private sector . . . in contrast to Whitehall's aid to British cities – relatively few strings were attached. It also seemed to consist in a frank realization that the days of the urban manufacturing economy were over, and that success consisted in finding and creating a new service-sector role for the central city. Bored suburbanites would come in droves to a restored city that offered them a quality of life they could not find in the shopping mall. Yuppies – or Young Urban Professionals – would gentrify the blighted Victorian residential areas close to downtown, and inject their dollars into restored boutiques, bars and restaurants. Finally, the restored city would actually become a major attraction to tourists, providing a new economic base to the city.[2]

The Baltimore project received $180 million of Federal funding plus $58 million from the city but only $22 million from the private sector. Both Baltimore and Boston benefited from the positive involvement of shrewd and determined city mayors whose input in the implementation process was crucially important. The downtown developments have now brought new life and employment to city centres which most people in America in the 1960s had written off – the large departmental stores

had been moved to the suburbs; the streets had become run-down, deserted and dangerous; few people ventured there at night. Some observers consider that the downtown developments have rescued the cities from the ultimate fate of the suburbanization of American society. To some extent they are right but, whilst there have been some splendid results in environmental and architectural terms, the developments have encouraged tourism rather than discouraged the net outward migration of people and employment.

Neighbourhood renewal and housing

The preservation of the inner-city residential neighbourhoods has shown that there is a viable urban alternative to living in suburbia. The history of housing in the USA since the late 1960s is full of examples where people in the inner cities have come together and fought to protect their neighbourhood and to campaign for the right to a decent home. Funding for neighbourhood revitalization has mainly been through Community Urban Development Action Grants (UDAGs) from the government's Department of Housing and Urban Development (HUD). Before approval was given, the communities had to show that the grant would attract at least 2.5 times as much private as public funding, and that the project could not be funded in any other way.[3]

There have been significant achievements in neighbourhood renewal in the USA. It has been one of the major forces in tackling the country's housing issues. The leading problem is the acute

18 *Infill housing which has been sensitively integrated into an existing residential neighbourhood in Pittsburgh.*

housing shortage but there is also the demographic change in the household structure – only one in ten American households are a standard family type with mother, father and children under 18. The majority of couples are having fewer or no children at all. Single people constitute a quarter of all households, and single parent families another 12 per cent.[4] More could have been achieved if housing were higher on the political agenda. There has never been any significant amount of public sector housing supported financially by the state or local government in the USA as in Britain and some other European countries, but assistance has been given in the form of tax deductions for mortgage interest for moderately priced ownership housing, and to assist

19 *Single room occupancy hostel, Los Angeles. Architects: Koning Eizenberg Architects.*

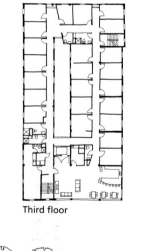

Third floor

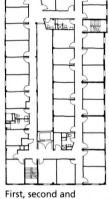

First, second and fourth floors

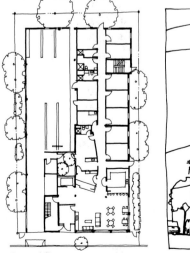

Ground floor

with rent (p. 54). These initiatives began in the 1960s under liberal presidents Kennedy and Johnson but regrettably were considerably curtailed under the Reagan and Bush administrations.

Furthermore, to assist in the provision of housing that is more accessible to poorer people, some city authorities require that a percentage of housing units in new developments be made available at below market rates to households who cannot afford market rates. The cost of this comes from the scheme as a whole (p. 00). If a supported dwelling is resold it must be to another income qualifying household. The original purchaser recovers their down payment, the principal amortization, and the depreciated value of improvements adjusted for inflation at the time of resale. Owners do not recover speculative profits regardless of how much the dwelling has appreciated. Another means is to link new housing to a commercial development (p. 57), in which case the developer places money into a housing trust fund to subsidize housing.

Homelessness and unemployment

Historically, single people on low incomes in the USA found refuge in lodging houses – Single Room Occupancy dwellings (SROs). Large numbers of these disappeared in the 1960s with the comprehensive redevelopment of inner-city areas. In their article on housing the homeless in the USA, published in *Built Environment*, Thomas P. Foder and Lois S. Grossman advised on the increasing use of 'Transitional Shelters' to help to alleviate the problem, and the revival of SROs to yield much needed accommodation for increasing numbers of homeless people.[5] They commented that, though the form of housing is simple, transitional shelters avoid the practice of dumping recently homeless people into standard housing projects, with all the accompanying social difficulties that can be created for them and other residents.

1 Quincy Market
2 Navy Yard

20 *Site and location plan of Quincy Market, Boston. Architects: Benjamin Thompson Associates.*

Instead, in addition to providing accommodation, the shelters offer programmes to build up self-sufficiency, self-esteem and supportive relationships.[5] Components of transitional programmes may include parenting and child development, home management, budgeting, nutrition, health, education, employment and career training, and counselling. SROs are multi-unit dwellings with small private rooms, private or common bathrooms and kitchen/living facilities (Fig. 19). Fodor and Grossman recognize the limitations of this accommodation but admit that it is better than no accommodation at all.[6]

Unemployment

Housing may be a large issue, but the overriding problem in American inner cities is the lack of work. Unemployment among black people is higher than amongst white people but according to Professor John Julius Wilson of Chicago University 'The trauma of persistent urban poverty is not automatically linked to racial issues . . . nothing will go right for the inner city, whether black or white, until the disease of joblessness is overcome. A job, at whatever level, links your family to the rest of society in a way that nothing else can.'[7] The alternative in so many American cities are youth gangs and drug dealings. The American ideology of work is not absent but there is simply no work available in inner-city areas where only 1 in 20 are employed.

Boston

Regeneration of waterfront areas

Boston was the first port in the United States of America to experience economic decline on the huge scale that was to become widespread in the 1970s and 1980s. In 1957 the Boston Redevelopment Authority was established to manage the redevelopment of the waterfront and by 1991 it contained a workforce of 300

Commercial Street

22 *Right: Quincy Market buildings, Boston.*

21 *Warehouses converted into condominiums in Boston's waterfront area – seen from St Columbus Park.*

23 Warehouses converted into offices and workshops, Cambridge, MA.

people.[8] The change began in the late 1950s with the redevelopment of Scollay Square, the run-down former maritime quarter and the construction of the new city hall and government complex in the centre of the city. This was followed in the mid-1970s by the refurbishment of the old harbourside Quincy Market buildings by architects Benjamin Thompson Associates (Fig. 20). This was linked to the present waterfront by the Walkway to the Sea and Columbus Park (Fig. 21) which was laid out on the site of demolished fishing sheds. A no less important feature of the regeneration was the refurbishment completed in 1992 of two of the city's landmarks, Faneuil Hall, built in 1742 and the old State House, built in 1713. The refurbishment of the Quincy Market buildings was the key to the Boston regeneration (Fig. 22) for geographically they were at the centre of activity in the city, they are close to the waterfront, the business district, the residential North End, the Government Center, and to several large hotels.

Boston is undoubtedly thriving. Today, the city authorities can demand virtually anything from developers. Generally they choose to demand lower building heights, richer details, better materials and public amenities – waterfront access, subway connections, and in the case of the recent Rowes Wharf development, a water taxi service.

The same process has been repeated in another, much less favourable part of Boston, across the Charles River at Cambridge. The area was once a centre for light manufacturing, but by 1970 it had become a no-man's land of vacant sites and empty warehouses, some of which have recently been refurbished and converted into offices, workshops and housing (Fig. 23). The area has now been significantly uplifted, both economically and physically through the construction of new housing and offices, and from the construction of the 'Galleria'. This

24 Charlestown Navy Dockyard, Boston.

comprises shopping on three levels overlooking a long internal atrium which opens out onto a crescent of further shops fronting on to a canal and an urban water park (Fig. 27).[9] The design of the development is an excellent example of the relationship between quality and commercial success.

Neighbourhood renewal and housing

The Boston Redevelopment Authority was very successful in negotiating a major housing component with commercial developers. The waterfront warehouses of

25 *New housing on the Charlestown waterfront.*

26 *Tent City, Boston.*

which the Boston City Council commissioned the preparation of a master plan for its future development. Most of the former barracks, which line a grid of roads, have now been converted into housing. Vacant sites have been infilled with new housing or have been planted to form new open space. The streets have been lined with trees which gives the whole place a somewhat European atmosphere (Fig. 24). Overlooking the waterfront are groups of new housing that would be at home in any European city (Fig. 25).

Tent City

The most significant low-income housing which has been built recently in Boston is Tent City. The fact that it was ever built demonstrates the power which the ordinary inner-city dweller in the USA can possess. The impetus for the development was a misguided redevelopment programme that cleared the site of housing to make way for a large-scale commercial development. The residents in the area protested against the demolition and demanded the redevelopment of part of the land with housing. They emphasized their protest by establishing a city of tents on the site. After 20 years of perseverance, in 1988, these activists saw the realization of their

the North End were refurbished into condominium apartments. New housing, in which the Authority was able to demand a percentage of low-income accommodation, matches the character of the old buildings. One of the most ambitious projects was at Charlestown Navy Yard. Charlestown is a Boston neighbourhood just across the mouth of the River Charles from the city's downtown area. The Navy Yard stretches along much of the Charlestown waterfront. Within the yard is the frigate USS *Constitution*, which attracts large numbers of people. The yard closed in 1970, after

27 *The Galleria, Cambridge, MA.*

housing goal. The project includes 269 residential units and 129 car parking spaces located on an adjacent (enclosed) piece of land. The design relates to the scale and character of the surrounding streets with building heights ranging from two to twelve storeys (Fig. 26). The density of 81.5 dwellings per acre is high, but this does not seem to deter the residents from enjoying the scheme. Entrance to the dwellings in the higher units is through a reception area which is controlled 24 hours a day through a concierge system. By the incorporation of retail shopping and a cafe at street level, together with community meeting rooms and daycare facilities, the project makes a positive impact on its neighbourhood.[10]

Baltimore

Inner Harbor

The Inner Harbor, which 20 years ago was a crumbling and dangerous wasteland, is now a waterside jewel of promenades and shopping pavilions. It is Baltimore's pride. The regeneration began in 1962 when the City Council declared a policy 'to return the shoreline to the people'.[11] The work began with the construction of waterside promenades and a dock for the frigate, *Constellation* (Fig. 28). By the mid-1970s a series of undistinguished office buildings had been placed in a row north of the water. The first major building was the 28-storey World Trade Center office tower by I. M. Pei. At about the same time a science centre, marina and ceremonial landing were built on the south side of the harbour at the foot of Federal Hill. Harborplace, the twin two-storey waterside pavilions containing shops, restaurants and associated uses, was completed in 1980. The two pavilions are at right angles to each other on the north and west shorelines. Between them is a stepped plaza which acts as a gateway to the Inner Harbor. The aquarium, which includes a tropical rain forest, was completed in 1981.

The basic approach to the design of the

pavilions by the architects, Benjamin Thompson Associates, was to create a lively urban scene – 'settings for festive human interaction' (Fig. 29).[12] The contribution of design to the commercial success of the development is clear. This resulted from a close working relationship between the architect and the developer, Jim Rouse of the Rouse Corporation. Benjamin Thompson commented in an article in *Building Design*, 'You listen – which is becoming more of a lost art – and try to find out as much as you can on all sides; not just architectural problems, but economic, social, conservation or anything-else problems. We don't look for easier path solutions or expect to see things repeated each time'.[13] The practice admits that working with some developers can be difficult: 'We're not friends with all developers. Some are led by accounting departments but we work with the ones with vision'.[14] Benjamin Thompson had the added advantage of first-hand knowledge of the retailing and restaurant world. For twenty years he ran his own shops, selling well-designed furniture and fabrics which gave him experience of what sold and to whom, and of the importance of detail in the design of commercially profitable spaces.

The redevelopment of the Inner Harbor has considerably increased Baltimore's tourist trade. The authorities claim that it attracts more than 18 million people every year, which is higher than the number of visitors to Disneyland. In employment terms the total number of jobs created by tourism rose from 16,000 in 1981 to 20,000 in 1984, and has continued to rise since then.[15]

Regeneration of residential neighbourhoods

A most important objective of Baltimore City Council's plan in 1964 was the refurbishment of the 200-year-old residential neighbourhoods at the perimeter of the Inner Harbor

28 *One of the pavilions at Baltimore's Inner Harbor, seen through the masts of the SS Constellation.*

redevelopment area – Otterbein and Federal Hill, which contained large numbers of fine old brick townhouses. These have now been refurbished through a programme of homesteading. Derelict houses built in the nineteenth century were sold for as little as a dollar a time to individual families on condition that they were rehabilitated within two years. To make it possible for them to undertake the building works, the homesteaders were able to borrow money from the Housing and Urban Development Department at low interest rates. The homesteading had a parallel in a programme for retail premises known as 'shopsteading'. To commemorate the completion of the work, a small monument has been erected which contains the words 'A tribute to the homesteaders, creators of the Otterbein Community, 1975–1985' (Fig. 30).

The streets in the Otterbein area have been beautifully repaved with stone cobbles and red bricks laid in traditional Boston herringbone pattern, trees have been planted, street lighting replaced with Victorian lamp-posts, and permit car parking marked out. The smaller cleared sites have been planted and children's play areas provided. The larger vacant sites have been redeveloped with two- and three-storey townhouse and apartment dwellings, the design of which relates closely to the existing street housing. The same pattern of change took place in the Federal Hill neighbourhood, except for the environmental works.

Further downstream at Fells Point a large area of nineteenth-century street houses have also been improved through homesteading. The stimulus here came from a single person (Mrs Fisher) who moved into the area in 1965. Firstly, she drew public attention to the issues threatening the area. Then she and other residents established an Architectural Preservation Society to oppose the routing of a major highway through the neighbourhood. The Society then formed the Historic Fells Point and Federal Hill Fund Inc., a non-profit, tax exempted organization, incorporated to operate exclusively for educational and charitable purposes in preserving both areas as National Historic Districts. Fells Point was not immediately designated as such, but Federal Hill was. It was not until 1973 that the highway proposals were officially

abandoned. In 1974, the City Council organized the preparation of plans for the revitalization of the area and representatives of community groups and organizations formed the Fells Point Planning Council. By that time, some houses had been boarded up for 15 years and the society was concerned that, once the road proposals had been abandoned, private developers would move in and begin to demolish them before the master plan was approved by the City Council. Therefore it was decided to press for Fells Point to be declared an Urban Renewal Area, and appropriate legislation was quickly introduced by the City Council. This gave the City Department of Housing and Community Development and the Fells Point Planning Council power to control major changes not in line with the neighbourhood plan. Houses which had been compulsorily purchased

29 *Layout of the pavilions at the Inner Harbor. Architects: Benjamin Thompson Associates.*

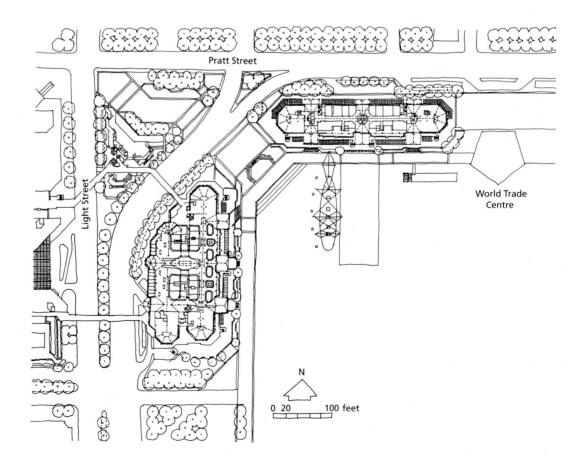

31 *Fells Point waterfront, Baltimore.*

by the City Council were offered back to their original owners. The main financial incentive for the homesteading was the facility to borrow money at a lower rate of interest from HUD. Some people gave up as the work was too much, but others succeeded and the area is now flourishing (Fig. 31).

Redevelopment in the Sandtown neighbourhood

The Inner Harbor and the Neighbourhood Regeneration have not in themselves solved Baltimore's inner-city problems. The hopes that the economic benefits of the Harbor development would trickle down to all have not become reality. In the neighbourhoods where there has been little or no investment there is overwhelming decline. 'It's clear that those investments have not uplifted the lives of people in some of the poorest neighbourhoods', claims Kurt Schmoke, the present Mayor of Baltimore. 'We'd like to concentrate on improvements in education and housing so that everybody will feel that regeneration.'[16] Several new projects are underway that, like the Inner Harbor, may become models for the country to follow. The plan for one

30 *Neighbourhood regeneration in the Otterbein district of Baltimore.*

of these projects, in the Sandtown neighbourhood, replaces eight tower blocks and similar high-rise blocks with low-rise housing elsewhere. The main aim is to break the concentration of poverty and racial segregation in these areas. The residents are almost all black and in receipt of welfare. Federal funding has been made available by President Clinton, without strings as to how it should be spent. James Rouse, the developer of the Inner Harbor, has been drawn into the partnership and he is the Chairman of the Enterprise Foundation, which is dedicated, he says, 'to ensuring fit and equitable housing for everyone within a generation'.[17] His foundation has given about $40 million in privately-raised funding for the Sandtown project, and provided much of the design and management expertise. At the beginning of 1993, however, the programme was handed over to a development corporation, majority managed by Sandtown residents.

The first project to benefit is in the Sandtown-Winchester neighbourhood. Here Baltimore will be the first city in the United States to demolish high-rise public housing wholesale; 227 new houses, subsidized with government funds and offered for sale at affordable weekly mortgage payments of $275, were recently completed. Children's play areas have been given new equipment and a mural known as 'Wall of Pride', depicting black American heroes from Bob Marley to Martin Luther King, has been repainted. Accompanying the new and rebuilt housing will be the creation of networks of social servicing, including health clinics and adult training centres.

The project is ambitious, but there are another 12 neighbourhoods in Baltimore with similar problems. Its critics say that too much money and effort is being concentrated in one area. It is, however, a landmark in the American approach to Urban Regeneration. Everything is being brought together to make the community work. It should show what could be achieved with the right injections of money. Only the politicians, directed by the voice of the people, will decide whether it can be repeated all over the country.

New York

South Street and Seaport Museum

The process for regenerating the downtown areas at Boston and Baltimore has been repeated in a number of other American cities. New York has Fulton Market and the South Street Seaport Museum (Fig. 32). The area was originally one of the former maritime quarters in the city, focusing on New York's food and fish markets surrounded by warehouses and counting houses. Between 1800 and 1870 it was the busiest part of the port of New York. By 1970 it had become very run-down.

The project was part of an urban master plan to restore a selected area of eleven blocks (Fig. 33). The development includes a new market building on the site of a demolished single-storey fish market constructed in 1953, a new pier building and a public plaza on reconstructed footings in the river. The special aims of the project were to reclaim the river edge for public use, to create open space amenities, activity, and to establish a setting for the museum's sailing ships. Benjamin Thompson Associates were appointed as the architects for the new Fulton Market and the adjacent Pier 17 development. Fulton Market is a four-sided building with a continuous cable-hung canopy on all four sides, which offers a measure of protection to outside food stands, cafe tables and pedestrians (Fig. 34). The form of the building and the materials were selected to relate to the refurbished nineteenth-century surroundings. Internally the building has four floors and a central atrium space.

The new Pier 17 building, completed in

1986, and the waterfront plaza are separated from the Fulton Market by an elevated highway that follows the river (Fig. 35). The building has been designed to reflect its maritime setting. Most of the shops, cafes and restaurants face inwards to a central atrium, but the design succeeds in achieving a good relationship between the inside and outside spaces through the numerous entrances and external staircases to upper floors, and the generous terraces and balconies (Fig. 37).

The project is extremely popular, but almost anything in such a location should have been a success. The major disappointment is to see that some of the buildings in the area are still dilapidated. The developers have limited their investments to certain of the blocks and it is a pity that the area has not been uplifted as a whole.

Housing

The overwhelming impression of New York is that in the inner areas beyond Manhattan the city is in a state of serious physical decline, with streets full of

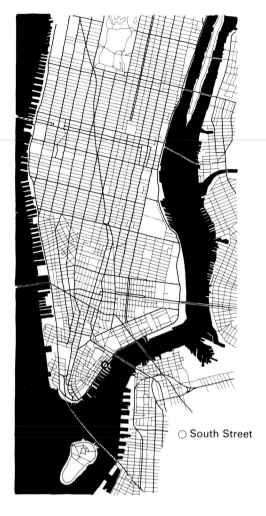

○ South Street

32 *Downtown waterfront, New York.*

33 *Above right: South Street Seaport, New York. Architects: Benjamin Thompson Associates.*

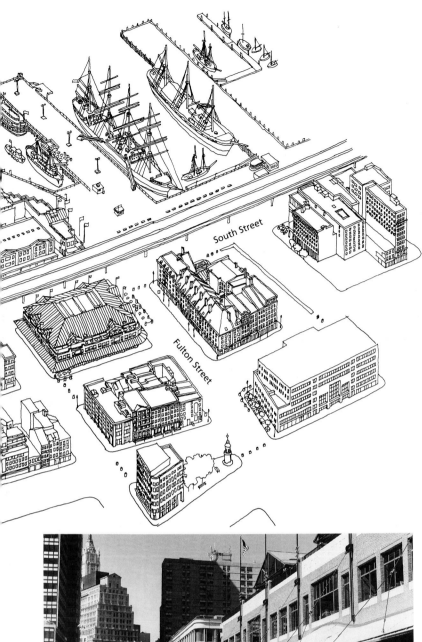

34 *Fulton Street Market, overlooked by the Manhattan skyline.*

daycare, medical offices, rooms for social services where the residents can be offered help and advice with child care or job counselling, and dining facilities. The residents remain in occupation until permanent housing can be found.[18]

Typical of the organizations that have been involved in providing housing for low income people is H.E.L.P. (Housing Enterprises for the Less Privileged), which has been very active in East New York. This non-profit-making organization not only manages the provision of housing and security for homeless people, but provides a full array of support services, and social interaction between the residents. One of their latest projects in Brooklyn occupies a full city block. The four-storey apartment building wraps around a courtyard and 'offers advantages that most New Yorkers would envy' (Figs 36 and 38).[19] The apartments are reached from outdoor balconies and stairways which are open to the courtyard. To encourage people to spend time on the balconies, the architects, Cooper Robinson and Partners, have made them wide enough for chairs and even a small table. The apartments themselves range from one-bedroom units of 54 sq. m. (575 sq. ft) in area to four-bedroom units of 114 sq. m. (1,225 sq. ft). The courtyard serves as a focal point: broken down into different zones, there is an active playground area and a variety of quiet outdoor areas (Fig. 39). With all 150 apartments looking on to the courtyard, there is plenty of surveillance to keep it safe. For security reasons, there is one single point of entry, which is controlled by a 24-hour concierge system. Entrance is through an octagon-shaped pavilion at one corner of the site fronting Blake Street. This was carefully located for reasons described by the project manager Don Lasker – 'We wanted people to enter the building from the part of the neighbourhood that's most intact'.[20] The connection with the existing community is also reinforced by linking a

derelict and semi-derelict buildings. Yet within these areas there exists an enormous will on the part of the people concerned with housing to make things better for the local communities. Homelessness is a severe problem. New York City Council has responded by building new 'transitional housing' projects on scattered sites throughout the city. The size of each project was limited to one hundred dwellings; all were provided with

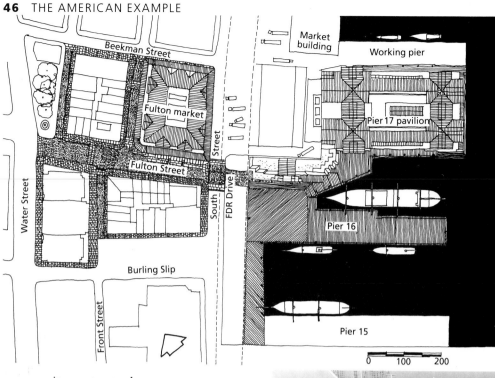

35 *Site plan of South Street Seaport, New York.*

36 *H.E.L.P.'s housing for low income and homeless people, East New York; looking into the central courtyard.*

37 *Above right: Pier 17, South Street Seaport.*

38 *Right: The quality of the design of H.E.L.P.'s housing is very high.*

community centre to the entrance area.

H.E.L.P. has not just built a very distinguished project, but through its sensitive management, it is establishing a good example for others to follow. Its management policies include ensuring a 50-50 split of the housing between black and white residents. There is also an innovative arrangement in which residents own shares of the management company itself and benefit from any savings in maintenance costs. This is designed to encourage upkeep by residents and a sense of community pride.

The same feeling of hope is to be seen in other streets nearby in which local church and other community groups have come together to build new housing in the form of simple terraces. Oscar Newman's defensible space principles are evident throughout the layout; every house has its own car parking space at the front protected by giant lion statuettes on the gate posts (Fig. 40).

Chicago

Housing

The contrast between the living conditions of the rich and poor in Chicago is extreme. At the upper end of society, the leafy suburbs of Oak Park in which Frank Lloyd Wright built his Prairie Houses at the turn of the century are symbolic of the American dream. At the lower end, the overriding impression of the city between the central area and the suburbs is one of

dereliction in which little of the former urban fabric still stands. However, Chicago's neighbourhood-based initiatives are bringing about the rebuilding of the abandoned housing, the resurrection of vacant factories and the revitalization of declining commercial areas. In recent years a concerted effort by the Department of Housing, the neighbourhood not-for-profit developers and their private sector partners has helped to save many abandoned buildings and stem further abandonment in targeted areas of the city. For example at West Garfield Park on Chicago's west side, Bethel New Life has been the catalyst for extensive housing investment and the provision of a full range of neighbourhood services, including a food cooperative, a health centre and an employment centre. Without the energy and the human resources of the neighbourhood groups such as this, 'the

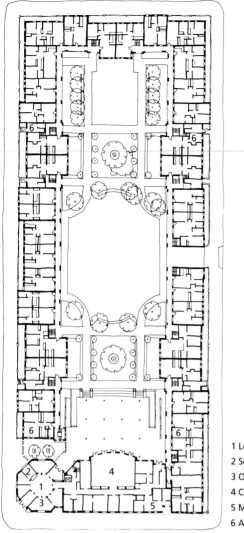

1 Lobby
2 Security
3 Office
4 Community
5 Medical suite
6 Apartment

39 Plans of H.E.L.P.'s housing. Architects: Cooper Robinson and Partners.

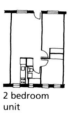

1 bedroom unit

2 bedroom unit

2 bedroom unit

3 bedroom unit

40 New street housing in East New York.

city could drift into a dangerous schism: the lakefront jewel and failing neighbourhoods'.[21]

Downtown regeneration

Chicago possesses a beautiful lakefront and 41 miles of rivers and canals, including the Chicago and Calumet River systems. They provide the city with a unique multi-use waterfront, giving a variety of scale and environment. In recent years, the areas around these waterfronts have become run-down and the buildings have become disused and derelict. One of the most recent developments which reflects the commercial potential of these areas is the North Pier where a former warehouse complex has been converted into a festival marketplace comprising speciality shopping, restaurants, night clubs, the Chicago Maritime Museum, and a Children's Museum (Fig. 41).

Pittsburgh

Regeneration of the Golden Triangle

The Allegheny and Monongahela Rivers, which join in Pittsburgh's downtown to form the Ohio River, divide the city into three roughly equal sections and provide 35 miles of river frontage within the city boundaries. The city centre fits into an area of land which has become known as the 'Golden Triangle' as a result of the amazing economic and physical transformation that took place after 1945 (Fig. 42). Seeing the disappearance of the steel industry which formed the original economy of the city, the business elite came together to revitalize the downtown area in order to prevent the collapse of the city's economy. An Urban Renewal Authority was set up in 1946. The first changes came about in the 1950s when smoke control regulations eliminated the major environmental blight of the steel-making process, which had given Pittsburgh its negative image. The

redevelopment of Gateway Centre, the USA's first urban renewal project, was a pump-primer which demonstrated the capacity and attractiveness of Pittsburgh as a business centre. This was followed by the clearance of derelict sites in the downtown area to accommodate the new headquarters of a number of major American corporations. In this way the city gained the position of USA's third-ranking business headquarters centre, which was remarkable for a city of its size (approx. 500,000 people). The development of new office space also reflected the start of a gradual shift in the region's economy from steel and heavy manufacturing to service and white-collar employment. The city became increasingly known for its financial institutions, hospitals and universities, such as Carnegie-Mellon and the University of Pittsburgh. Thus, its overall economy recovered and much of the built environment in the centre was renewed.

Building preservation

The preservation of old buildings has been an important part of the urban regeneration process in Pittsburgh. In 1964, the Pittsburgh History and Landmarks Foundation was established with the purpose of demonstrating that a practical approach to historic preservation could save individual old buildings and entire neighbourhoods, not merely the architecture of the neighbourhoods: but the usefulness of the buildings and the morale of the people who use them. In the view of the Foundation, preservation had to be related to the everyday world and the uses that the buildings could be put to. In the first 15 years of its existence, Landmarks concentrated on acquiring run-down houses in northside and southside neighbourhoods, and restoring them prior to resale, to set an example for others to follow. Thereafter it turned its attention to commercial revitalization and saw the need to press for the preservation of the old

buildings in the city centre as part of the urban renewal process. It was instrumental in securing the refurbishment of the Daniel Burnham building at Station Square as part of the development of a speciality shopping centre and office development. The Foundation now concentrates on education and promotion of preservation but it continues to use its funds on a revolving basis to support neighbourhood groups to undertake preservation projects.

The most important building to be renovated in recent years is the old Union Station, also designed by Daniel Burnham and built in 1890 (Fig. 43). The station contained a large amount of potential space in an office tower above the main station area, a rotunda in the forecourt of the building which served as a *porte-cochère* and railway sheds on the sides of the building. The city, through the Urban Redevelopment Authority, took out a bank loan to purchase the building and plans were drawn in 1982 for its restoration and conversion to new uses. Financing thereafter proved difficult but now the refurbishment is complete and Pittsburgh has a building of great delight.

Open space

The construction of several riverside parks in key locations in the 1970s (in one of which was located the Three Rivers Stadium) were important to the regeneration process as they helped to green the city's image. Frequently the development of the riverside parks came as part of the development package for an adjacent office or retail development.

41 *Above left: North Pier, Chicago.*

42 *The Golden Triangle, Pittsburgh.*

Urban design

Another important aspect of Pittsburgh's revival has been the recognition of the place of urban design in the process. The principles adopted are explained by Jonathan Barnett in an article entitled 'Urban design as a survival tool'[22], in which he advises that there are four ways in which urban design can help to determine a city's competitive edge:

1 Quality: Cities can do an enormous amount to improve their quality of life. It is important to encourage conventions and tourism, improve downtown retailing and speciality restaurants, encourage downtown housing and preserve residential neighbourhoods. Most successful cities have a major stadium, a symphony orchestra, a season of opera, at least one repertory theatre, a ballet and a

university important enough to sponsor lectures, concerts and other events involving nationally-known figures.

2 Transport: Good links to the national road network, adequate car parking downtown and efficient public transport.

3 Open space: Parks, plazas and public open space are significant factors in the quality of urban life. Important too are interior public spaces that are created as part of commercial development (e.g. the atrium and winter garden at PPG Place designed by Philip Johnson) (Fig. 44). How these spaces relate to each other and to the street system can make the city much easier and more pleasant to walk around in, which in turn benefits shops and offices.

4 Street furniture: Finally, seemingly trivial matters such as the design of street lights, signs and traffic signals, the paving to the sidewalks and streets plus the presence of street trees can make an enormous overall improvement in the character of a city.

Neighbourhood renewal and housing

In 1977 the City Council extended its urban regeneration activities to include the residential neighbourhoods in the inner areas, using public funding to assist housing rehabilitation and neighbourhood commercial revitalization as well as financing improvements to infrastructure and public facilities.

Pittsburgh is a city that is rooted in its residential neighbourhoods. Many people live in the same city area as their parents and even their grandparents. Over the past few years, community organizations have been working with city agencies to bring a new image to the older districts. The refurbishment of the houses and the construction of new houses in their neighbourhoods on small infill sites has

43 *The refurbished Union Street Station, Pittsburgh. The building was originally designed in 1890 by Daniel Burnham.*

been the principal means by which people have maintained this social fabric. HUD funding has been extensively available. In the streets around the Allegheny Center to the north of the downtown, and spreading out to the Manchester district, the developments are significantly improving the quality of the environment (Fig. 17). Most of the new housing is urban in style (Fig. 6), which contrasts to the more prevalent lower-density, single-unit development that is being built on infill sites in the neighbourhoods further out from the city centre.

A housing development which demonstrates the determination of the Pittsburgh Redevelopment Authority to encourage the regeneration of the inner-city neighbourhoods is at Crawford Square. Located at the edge of the downtown area of the city (Fig. 45), the 18-acre development revises the original street grid (Fig. 46). The project contains a mixture of two- and three-storey apartments, town houses and single-family houses (Fig. 47). The design of each street is carefully considered in relationship to guidelines produced by the architects, UDA of Pittsburgh. These specify materials and colours, as well as the design of bay windows, dormers, and fences. All have front and rear gardens (Fig. 48).

The scheme, which is intended for an economically mixed population with a wide range of incomes, comprises 350 rental units and 150 houses for sale. The details of the financial support given to the

44 *Public 'Winter Garden' at PPG Place, Pittsburgh.*

people who rent or buy the dwellings illustrate the aid that can be available to people in inner-city areas in the USA. For the people who purchase their home HUD offers approximately 25 per cent tax relief on mortgages, provided their income does not exceed $36,200 per year. However, repayment must be made to HUD upon sale, lease, or transfer of any interest in the property, unless HUD accepts that there is undue hardship. The rental terms also depend upon income. Of the first phase of 203 dwellings, 101 are eligible for affordable rental provided the applicant 'meets Federal eligibility guidelines relating to maximum income levels and have good credit rating'. The assistance means that affordable rents can be as much as 30 to 40 per cent less than the market rate. The maximum income limits allowed by HUD are for a one person household, $15,204 and for a five person household, $23,458. The HUD funding is administered through a locally established community development association and there is a Homeowners Association set up to organize community development and common maintenance, for which there is a small compulsory payment.[23]

St Louis

Downtown regeneration

'St Louis has gone from a symbol of civic decline to something of a model of a city pulling itself back together.'[24] By the late 1960s, the image of St Louis had plummeted. The population had declined from 850,000 in 1930 to 420,000. The city's tax base had been eroded, crime had increased, and the quality of public schools had declined.[25] City neighbourhoods – some of the oldest housing in the mid-west – continued to deteriorate until many were virtually abandoned. Rubble-strewn vacant lots and boarded-up stores became all too familiar. Sections of downtown became like ghost towns whilst office developments sprouted in the suburbs.

45 *Crawford Square housing. The form and density of the housing contrasts strongly with its downtown backcloth.*

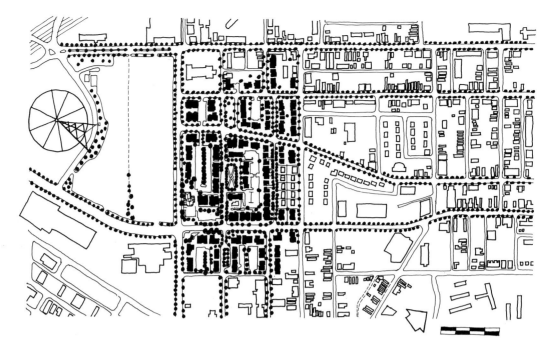

46 *Crawford Square housing: site layout.*

Apartment
Unit F1

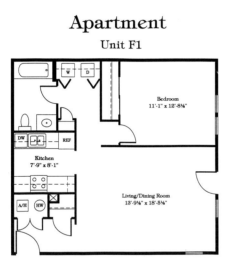

47 *Crawford Square housing: selection of house type plans.*

Townhouse
Unit B

1st Floor

2nd Floor

3rd Floor

3rd Floor
2nd Option

48 *Perspective of the Crawford Square housing development. Architects: UDA Architects, Pittsburgh.*

The turnround was not easily achieved and the process is still ongoing. The pattern is typical of many American cities. The first steps were taken in the 1960s, with the demolition of 40 riverside blocks of cast-iron buildings (an act that would likely not be repeated today) to create the Jefferson National Expansion Park along the river. Within this park Eero Saarinen's magnificent arch was constructed in 1965 which was to become the symbol of a new St Louis (Fig. 50).

As in Pittsburgh, the stimulus came from a small group of civic-minded leaders – two or three dozen business executives and academics, doctors and developers, bankers and politicians – whose first concern was to re-energize the city's downtown area and with this its economic base. Their group, called Civic Progress, formed the non-profit Civic Center Redevelopment Corporation to build a new stadium. Of utmost importance to the project's success was the state's Chapter 353 redevelopment tool, under which a city could pass to a developer real estate tax relief – that is, property taxes would be retained at the redevelopment level for 10 years and at half the newly assessed value for the next 15 years. In this way, the city government established and maintained an economic climate in which the private developer was prepared to take risks.[26] The construction of the stadium (completed in 1963) and the arch sparked new interest in the downtown and over the years to follow the area was transformed. None of the new buildings were allowed to exceed the height of the arch which today gives St Louis a very different atmosphere to most other major American cities.

Union Station

The most impressive downtown project is the conversion of St Louis station (built in 1894), which combines new construction and the renovation of the largest single-span train shed in the world. The development comprises a retail centre with a shopping mall, restaurants, a 550-room hotel, and a large pool built beneath the train shed roof. Completed in 1985, the financial packaging revolved around a $10 million UDAG and qualification of the entire project for a 25 per cent historic preservation tax credit. The refurbishment has produced a most exciting space, which is light and spacious (Fig. 51).[27,28] It is making a significant impact on the revival of the downtown area of St Louis.

Neighbourhood renewal and housing

As the decisions were being made on the downtown area, attention was also being directed to the many dilapidated residential neighbourhoods. The city realized by the early 1970s that it had to create additional incentives to lure private developers: federal monies for housing projects were supplemented by low-interest or no-interest loans as a one-time subsidy of the developer's costs. Eventually, loans were to be repaid to the city. The city's 'For Sale Incentive Program' was created to provide financial assistance to buyers. Together, the two programmes helped finance the construction and rehabilitation of more than 10,000 housing units (Fig. 49). By 1985, the city's Community Development Agency had received 28 Urban Development Action Grants (UDAGs) worth $78.7 million. Since then funding has been limited by the national government, but the process is still very alive.

Typical of the new development is Westminster Place (Fig. 52). The Westminster neighbourhood, which is close to the centre of St Louis, had severely deteriorated and become vice-ridden. Strongly supported by the City of St Louis, developers McCormac, Baron and Associates have transformed 15 square street blocks. The construction of the new housing and the refurbishment of the few remaining houses began in 1986. The

49 *Neighbourhood regeneration in St Louis.*

scheme comprises a mixture of rental apartments and houses, and houses for sale. The development was assisted commercially by the construction on adjacent land of a 50,000 sq. ft (4,600 sq. m.) supermarket which in itself contributes to the revival of the area. The design of Westminster Place is different to the developments in similar locations in other American cities featured in this book, but it is not an uncommon form of inner-city urban regeneration in the USA. The houses have a traditional American feel but the layout is suburban. There are good reasons for this. The single-family house and garage is popular in city neighbourhoods for the same reason that it appeals to people in the suburbs; its associations with the good life runs deep in American culture. Also the suburban 'tract' houses are the American building industry standard, no matter where they are built. In some city neighbourhoods the cost of land, which tends to keep density high, has fallen to a point where it is comparable to suburban sites. The suburban house is inherently more difficult to relate to existing buildings in the older neighbourhoods, but the resultant development is nevertheless attractive to the people who would otherwise choose to move to the suburbs.[29]

San Francisco

Waterfront regeneration

San Francisco has a distinctively European feel. Its streets reflect the urban quality found in many cities in France, Germany and Italy. It was the first city in the USA to recognize the potential of its waterfront area. In the 1950s the Fisherman's Wharf area contained large derelict warehouses and the area was rapidly declining. It now attracts 12 million visitors a year. The revitalization of Ghirardelli Square, in which the oldest building was constructed in 1864, was America's first urban adaptive re-use of old buildings to form a 'speciality retail centre' (Figs. 53 and 54). The complex, completed in the early 1960s, is strategically placed near the waterfront terminus of one of the cable car routes from the city centre and enjoys magnificent views over the bay beyond. The Cannery (Fig. 55), a building dating from the 1890s, was originally a Del Monte fruit packing plant. Today it is a three-storey complex of more than 50 shops, restaurants, galleries, and a cinema. Magicians, jugglers, comics, musicians, and other artists perform in the tree-shaded courtyard. The significance of these two developments is that they set off the wave of urban renovations in the downtown areas of cities across the USA. 'With Ghirardelli Square, people began to think that public environment could in some way reach out and touch people'.[30]

Housing

Fisherman's Wharf was so instrumental in raising the general appeal of the area that there was great pressure to build new housing along what was once a derelict waterfront, and on the hills above. The renewal of the Embarcadero began in the late 1950s with a competition sponsored by the San Francisco Redevelopment Agency, which resulted in a mixture of four residential towers and two-storey

51 *A new light and spacious interior exists beneath the world's largest single-span railway shed at St Louis.*

50 *Left: The magnificent Saarinen arch was the inspiration for urban regeneration in St Louis.*

52 *Westminster Place, St Louis: low-density housing which is typical in many American inner-city areas.*

53 *Ghirardelli Square, San Francisco was the first 'Festival Marketplace' in the USA.*

town houses. However, three city blocks were not developed under the original plan due to the changes in housing demand and the objections of the local residents (Fig. 56). The public pressure was so intense that, for the first time in San Francisco, the developers were forced to build low-rise housing that related to its surroundings.

Golden Gateway Commons

The development for the three vacant blocks which resulted from this pressure was Golden Gateway Commons, designed by architects Fisher-Freidman Associates. This medium-rise, mixed-use development contains shops and cafes on two floors, and three storeys of housing above. The shops open on to an arched colonnade and pavement cafes face the well-used Sidney Walton Park. The brick vernacular, scale and detailing is far more in keeping with the character of the area than the high-rise development built in earlier years. The housing is grouped around landscaped courtyards at second-floor level (Fig. 57). 'The major accomplishment of Golden Gateway Commons is that it creates an enclave with intimately scaled garden spaces in the heart of a city while contributing to urban streetscape'.[31]

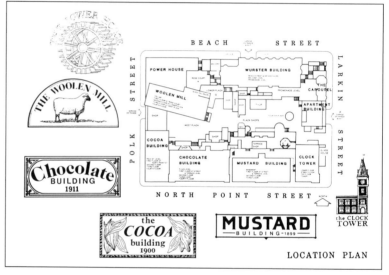

54 *Site plan of Ghirardelli Square, San Francisco. Architects: Benjamin Thompson Associates.*

Delancy Street: housing for young offenders

Whilst most recent housing along the Embarcadero has been built for young professionals and families, some effort is being made by the City Authorities to meet the wider needs of people in the inner city (Fig. 58). Close by to Golden Gateway Commons is the Delancy Street housing for the 'hardcore hopeless who need a last chance to clean up their lives'.[31]

The project was developed by the Delancy Street Foundation, which is a self-financing organization that is independent of public funding – the money for its work coming from the

55 *The Cannery, San Francisco.*

56 *Golden Gateway Commons, San Francisco, seen adjacent to the earlier high-rise development.*

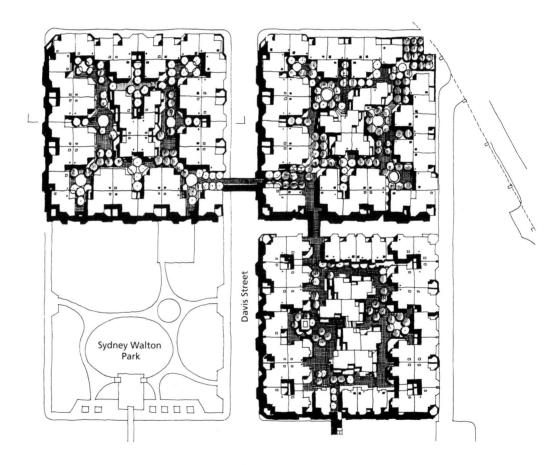

Davis Street

Sydney Walton Park

57 *Golden Gateway Commons: site layout at podium level.*

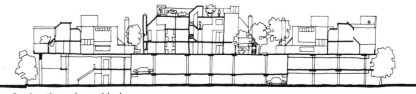

Section through one block

income-producing businesses that are run by the occupants themselves. The development is intended for young people who are recovering from drug or alcoholic addiction, or have committed serious crimes. To stay in the development, they will have agreed to learn social and working skills, take vocational training, and work successfully in the community – without payment – for a minimum period of time. The shortest stay is two years, but most live there for much longer. The senior residents help the new people to rehabilitate themselves in 'bootstrap' fashion. The development contains 177 two-bedroom apartments, food service, shops and workspaces for the income-producing businesses, a 500-seat assembly hall, a 150-seat film room, a swimming pool and a fitness centre. Around the perimeter of the site, at ground level, are public retail shops including a 400-seat restaurant operated by the residents (Fig. 59).

The project was designed with the full participation of the residents by architects Backen, Arrigoni and Ross, and was built as a cooperative venture between the San Francisco Building Trades Council, Apersey Construction and the Delancy Street residents, using many donated materials and services – but no public money was sought. The involvement of the residents has not reduced the quality of the scheme or the workmanship. In an article in *Architectural Record*, Charles Linn quoted the view of the architects as follows: 'In terms of the technical work, they were the equal to any contractor I've ever worked with, primarily because all of those working on [the project] were very smart, and very much into building a really good building. They wanted it to be right and it shows'.[32]

There is much that can be learnt from this project about building special needs housing in inner cities. The architect advises 'there is always a temptation to institutionalize – not to add that little bit

of detail, so you can put on another room, and try and maximize the number of people you can warehouse. Delancy Street works because it doesn't do that. These people are just like other human beings. How comfortable can we make them? How much light and air should be in the space? These should be no different here than they are in any other high-quality housing project. Everybody is trying to figure out why it works. The bottom line is that Delancy Street is a damned nice place to be'.[33]

Mendelsohn House

Mendelsohn House, a 189-dwelling apartment complex for low-income elderly people, reflects another long struggle by a local community to prevent their being uprooted by developers. The building and its community garden are a monument to

58 *Housing for former young offenders at Delancy Street, San Francisco waterfront.*

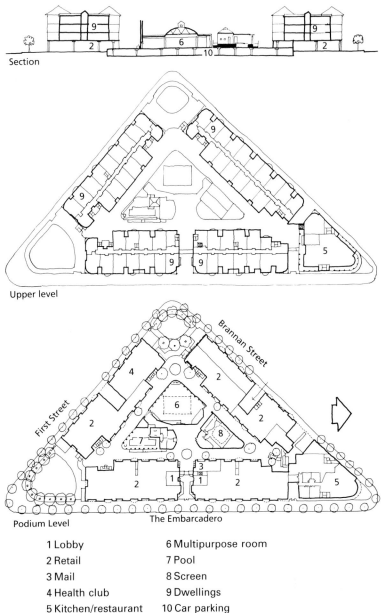

Section

Upper level

Brannan Street

First Street

The Embarcadero

Podium Level

1 Lobby
2 Retail
3 Mail
4 Health club
5 Kitchen/restaurant
6 Multipurpose room
7 Pool
8 Screen
9 Dwellings
10 Car parking

59 *Plans of the Delancy Street housing. Architects: Backen, Arrigoni and Ross.*

one of the most determined pieces of citizen activity to occur in any American city in recent years.

In the 1950s, the South Market area of San Francisco became a prime target for the demolition of the existing residential area with its rooming houses (SROs), and the construction of large-scale commercial development on the cleared sites. The residents, including the single elderly men who lived in the rooming houses – some of whom were retired trade unionists – were not to be moved without a fight. By 1973 the group which they established, the Tenants and Owners in Opposition to Redevelopment (TOOR), had won a settlement through the courts requiring the San Francisco Redevelopment Agency to provide at least 1500 units of relocation housing for residents in the area and set aside four sites for housing built by non-

profit-making groups, to be partially funded by raising the city's hotel tax. Mendelsohn House, designed by architects Robert Herman Associates, is the third of the four projects that were planned.

The complex of studio and one-bedroom apartments are in a nine-storey block fronting the main road, Folsom Street, and in seven- and three-storey wings at the rear which enclose a central courtyard. The lower blocks are located on the south side, to ensure the maximum penetration of sunlight into the internal courtyard (Fig. 60). On the ground floor are common rooms, a lounge, a community dining room, a multi-purpose room with a television, an exercise and arts room, and a neighbourhood health centre. An emergency alarm call system links the apartments to the main desk and the manager's apartment. Open arcades

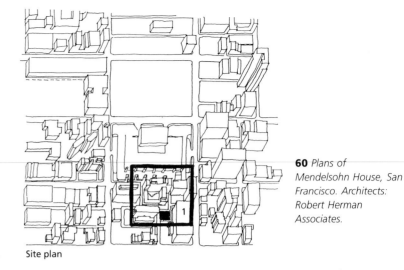

beneath the lowest block at the rear of the development link the project to the surrounding neighbourhood; nearby is a well-used community garden with shaded seating areas and small raised beds in which the residents plant their flowers and vegetables (Fig. 61).[34]

Mission Bay

The largest urban regeneration project in San Francisco is the redevelopment of Mission Bay. Located less than a mile south-east of the centre of San Francisco's financial district, the site was formerly marshalling yards, terminals and piers for rail and boat shipping. The site has a two-mile shoreline overlooking San Francisco Bay. Various proposals for the redevelopment of the land have been prepared since the late 1970s and it is only recently that an agreement between the city authorities and the local community has been reached on the basis of plans prepared by a consortium of architects including Skidmore, Owings and Merrill and local architect Daniel Solomon. The agreement has only come about following the willingness of the City Authorities to assume control of the planning process and to put itself in the driving seat not only for determining the appropriate development but also for seeking community consensus for the plan. The developer, the Santa Fe Pacific Reality Corporation (later renamed the Catellus Development Corporation) agreed to donate $2 million for planning purposes.

There are five objectives of the plan (Fig. 62):

1 Mixed Uses. The project is to accommodate 8000 houses, offices and other uses to generate employment.

2 Urban Design. The design is to extend street and building patterns from adjacent neighbourhoods, and should reflect the need for appropriate urban densities to be

1 Alice Street Gardens
2 Adult day health centre
3 Exercise / arts
4 Dining area
5 Lounge
6 Multi-use
7 Residential

First floor

Ground floor

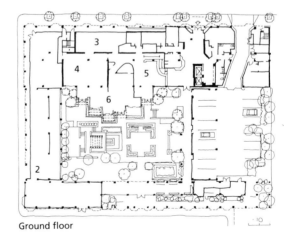

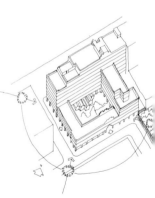

62 *Mission Bay development plan. Architects: Skidmore, Owings and Merrill with Daniel Solomon Associates.*

N   0   500   1000 ft

achieved. This would maximize the benefit of the high level of public transport available in the area.

3   As much as 30 to 40 per cent of the housing should be subsidized below market rents and sale prices through tax incentives.

4   All infrastructure costs should be borne by the developer.

5   There should be significant waterfront access provided for residents.

The community consultation process absorbed a tremendous amount of time and effort, as over 50 or more civic organizations were involved at one time or another. Community groups were involved in setting the programme for the planning work, in selecting the consultants, in the preparation of the objectives and policies statement, in drafting the plan, and in the examination of the Environmental Impact Report. In addition to the official public hearings, the City Council held a two-day

workshop to explore the consultant's plan, and alternative plans drawn up by three community groups. The involvement of the community paid off in that there is now a consensus of agreement, but the planning process took five years rather than the 18-month period originally envisaged.[35]

61 *Left: Mendelsohn House seen through the community gardens.*

3 The British practice

Emergence of the problems

The first public recognition of the need for urban regeneration in Britain came in 1972 when Peter Walker, the Secretary of State for the Environment, set consultants to work in three deprived inner-city areas in Lambeth, Liverpool and Birmingham. The results of these studies and the subsequent Government White Paper in 1977 underlined the acute level of deprivation in the inner city. The Inner Urban Area Act, 1978, gave rise to the Urban Programme by which the government switched its financial resources from new towns to urban areas to help the cities. The first half of the following decade saw a gradual, but slow, focusing of public attention on the issues. Riots in Brixton (London), Toxteth (Liverpool), and Moss Side (Manchester) in 1981, followed in 1985 by further disorders in Handsworth (Birmingham) and Broadwater Farm (London) caused significant public concern. In 1985, the Archbishop of Canterbury's group published their report *Faith in the City*,[1] which highly condemned the government policies in the inner cities. The Prime Minister, Mrs Thatcher, finally embraced the problems of inner cities as a major part of government policy when in 1987 she stood on a derelict site in Teeside vowing that action would be taken.

Government intervention

Forms of intervention
Since 1981 there has been a wide variety of government intervention, most of which has been directed towards encouraging private sector involvement. There have also been a large number of funding measures and agencies established to support these approaches:

63 *Looking towards the City of London over the roofs of the new housing in the Surrey Docks.*

1 Derelict Land Grants for the reclamation of derelict land and buildings, to create sites suitable for development and to provide landscaped open space.

2 Urban Development Corporations (UDCs), which are the urban counterpart of New Town Development Corporations of the 1960s and 1970s, set up by the government to intervene where it considers that the existing local authorities are unable to act effectively.

3 Enterprise Zones (EZs), which are a device to stimulate industrial and commercial development by virtue of looser development control and tax relief.

Within an Enterprise Zone:

* Developers can offset their building costs against Income Tax or Corporation Tax. The taxpayer thereby subsidizes the construction costs of any buildings.

* There are no planning controls. An authority is designated under the legislation as the 'zone authority', but normal planning permission is not required. This allows flexible use of buildings. Shells can be constructed and the use modified to suit the most profitable market. For developers it therefore helps minimize risk and maximize profit.

* Businesses are exempt from local taxation for the 10 years' duration of the Enterprise Zone. The government makes the payment to the local authority. While this may not directly profit the developer it does mean that higher than average rents can be charged, which increases the value of the development. The largest Enterprise Zone is in the Isle of Dogs.[2]

4 City Challenge, introduced in 1991, which has now replaced most of the previous funding methods to local authorities and private sector companies (except for Derelict Land Grants). This involves the 'top-slicing' of 82.5m a year of inner cities and housing programme funding from 1992–3 to 1996–7.[3] City Challenge requires the development of a strategy which relates the area in question to the larger city economy, and the involvement of the widest range of local organizations and private sector organizations in its preparation and implementation. The funding is made available on a competitive basis between local authorities. It is this competitive element which has given so much cause for concern but the concept of local authorities, with the private sector, community groups etc., preparing an overall strategy for one or more of their inner-city areas is very sound.

5 Task Forces, which are small groups of professionals, seconded from central and local government and the private sector, based locally and charged with stimulating business enterprise, employment and environmental upgrading.

6 City Action Teams, which have responsibilities similar to that of Task Forces. The difference relates to the availability of cross (government) departmental funding, whereas the funding for Task Forces comes only from the Department of Trade and Industry.

7 Training and Enterprise Councils (TECs). Eighty-two TECs and 22 Scottish counterparts have been formed to channel funds totalling over £2 billion into training schemes for both the employed and unemployed. The TECs are required to undertake a full assessment of the local training supply and needs, taking account of the special needs and equal opportunities issues. They are also responsible for managing some industry-education links through Education Business Partnerships.

8 The Enterprise Initiative, which offers inner-city businesses help to improve their performance. Firms of under 500 employees can have grants for consultancy projects to improve marketing, design, quality of product and manufacturing processes.

9 Local Enterprise Agencies, which are companies limited by guarantee and managed by a Board drawn from their sponsors. These include major companies as well as local firms. Their main activity is to give free advice to new and existing businesses.

10 The Safer Cities Programme, which operates in 16 areas, involving over 650 local crime prevention schemes.[4]

11 Estate Action and Housing Action Trusts (HATs) for the regeneration of local authority housing estates.

12 Garden Festivals, which were once an important feature of the government's urban regeneration programme, but now, regrettably, have been discontinued. Liverpool, Glasgow, Gateshead, Stoke-on-Trent and Ebbw Vale were all beneficiaries.

The concentration of action through this proliferation of semi-autonomous and/or centrally accountable institutions has somewhat diluted the role of local authorities. This represents a major shift in the interest and power structure within inner-cities policy.[5] Some observers say that the number of interventions and agencies involved is bewildering and that it lacks cohesion, whilst others justify them on the basis that each carries out a relatively separate and specific function which is of a size and level of magnitude that can be grasped by a manageable group of people.

National Urban Regeneration Agency

The latest solution to the lack of cohesion is the government's establishment of a National Urban Regeneration Agency (NURA) (now known in England as 'English Partnerships'). The agency will embrace all the means of funding previously available and act as facilitator to local government, the urban development corporations, the HATs, Estate Action and the private sector. Its budget will be administered through integrated regional offices combining the departments of the Environment, Employment, Transport and Trade and Industry. Introduced in April 1994, it should be able to provide more substantial funds than previously available to a single agency. It is hoped that this will ensure a more flexible and a more focused approach to solving inner-city problems.

The possibility of a central agency has existed since 1977. The idea was the cornerstone of an inner-city report published by the Royal Institute of British Architects in 1987.[6] However, the idea is not without its critics. In 1989, the Audit Commission saw an agency as unrealistic, because of the widely different problems which needed to be tackled in different parts of the country.[7] A national agency might help to focus on the issues but experience with similar national bodies that already exist, e.g. the Housing Corporation, suggests that it could easily become too bureaucratic, and lacking independence from central government interference, to be really effective in achieving the level of quality that is needed.

The Urban Development Corporations

There are currently eleven Urban Development Corporations (UDCs) in

England and Wales – London Docklands, Merseyside, Trafford Park, Cardiff Bay, Black Country, Teeside, Tyne and Wear (Fig. 64), Central Manchester, Leeds, Sheffield and Bristol. There is also the Laganside Development Corporation in Belfast, Northern Ireland. These have responsibility for uplifting the former industrial areas in the centre of each city. Their designated areas are all related to significant water features such as former docks, rivers, sea, estuaries or canals. They have planning (development control) and compulsory purchase powers, which has made them the owners of much of the land in their designated areas. The same powers of compulsory land acquisition have generally been denied to local authorities since 1979.

Government funding to the UDCs in 1991–2 totalled £470m. This enabled them to purchase and reclaim land, improve the environment and encourage development.[8] £225 million of this was spent on the London Docklands, which represents 50 per cent of the Department of the Environment's (DOE) urban expenditure.

The UDCs frequently receive criticism for being non-democratic. Most are now trying to remedy this by developing close links with the local authorities and people living and working in the area. The Town and Country Planning Association is in favour of development corporations but recommends a number of changes to their management and control which would certainly help to make them more welcome. These are as follows:

1 UDCs should only be set up within a particular inner city if the local authority agrees.

2 UDCs should be required to produce a publicly-agreed planning and development strategy for their areas which must be related to the planning strategies for the whole of the surrounding urban area.

3 UDCs should be obliged by their terms of reference to set up an ongoing consultation process with local people so as to determine their needs and wishes.

4 UDC boards should have a small majority of their members drawn from the local authorities for that area.[9]

The principal criticism the UDCs (also HATs and Estate Action) face is that they are being funded from a top-slicing of the money that previously would have been available to local authorities to spend on their priorities. The problem is aggravated by the continual reduction in the

64 *Riverside regeneration in Newcastle-upon-Tyne.*

government's grant allocation to local authorities which, in turn, is causing the decline of ordinary municipal services such as schools, health, social welfare, council housing, and, above all, the maintenance of the public realm. In addition, there is a continual reduction in the amount each year that local authorities can spend on their own housing stock. The UDCs are not, therefore, seen as an additional resource with which local authorities can work in partnership but rather as an intruder, unnecessarily taking over the role that they could play if they were allowed to spend the money available to the UDCs. The opponents of this view

suggest that the local politicians would disperse the money for their own short-term political gain, rather than concentrate it on key issues. However, partnership, which the government is keen to promote, would be more meaningful to local authorities if the public sector spending rules were changed and borrowing, financed locally, stopped counting against public sector spending limits. Local authorities could then act with the private sector on a more equal basis. This would also enable them to build housing for social need. In no other country in the western world does central government exercise so much control over local affairs.

Waterside development

The successes and failures of British urban regeneration policy have been nowhere better illustrated than in the various dockside and riverside developments that have taken place in the last few years. With the exception of a few notable examples – Salford, Swansea and Hull – most of the large waterfront projects have been initiated by the Urban Development Corporations. A common feature of the developments is the mixture of uses in the same location. This includes housing, offices, workshops and small factory/ warehouse units, hotels, leisure buildings such as cinemas and bowling alleys, cafes and restaurants. The design quality of the projects varies, although there has clearly been no shortage of finance for infrastructure works. New roads, renovated dock walls, river and canal banks, and lock gates, and large quantities of tree and shrub planting abound. In some places, great efforts have been made to refurbish the nineteenth-century warehouses and other buildings, and to convert them into new uses (Fig. 65). It is regrettable that there is very little social housing. This reflects the market-led approach to urban generation in Britain. Funding from public sources is largely only available to support private sector development and a small amount by housing associations. The social tasks are concerned with bringing derelict land back into use and in this way to strengthen the urban economy as a whole. Few of the projects have had any objectives which involve a local community. Few to date have had a significant impact on the problems of poverty and unemployment in the wider area in which they are located. The people there can only hope to benefit indirectly from the new jobs created until the problems of the wider city are resolved. Nevertheless, despite this, the developments themselves can now begin to be appreciated.

65 *Warehouse conversions in Cardiff.*

Urban villages

The latest solution to the redevelopment of derelict inner-city land is the design of 'urban villages'. The concept has received the approval of Prince Charles, who has been considerably outspoken in recent years on architecture and urban design since his 1984 'carbuncle' speech at Hampton Court, London. In 1989 he published *A Vision of Britain*,[10] but his most significant contribution to urban regeneration was the publication of *Urban Villages* in 1992.[11] Although much criticized by the architectural world in Britain, many of the recommendations are attractive. The concept in respect of inner cities is that urban villages are a means of regenerating derelict land on a sustainable, human scale. They are the antithesis of rigid, top-down, master planning, in which commercial criteria can all too easily dictate, rather than respond to, social and economic criteria.

The main principles are as follows:

1 Multi-use development in 40-hectare (100-acre) neighbourhoods with a resident population of between 3000–5000.

2 There should be mixed uses within each street block as well as within the village.

3 Houses and flats should balance workspace so as to achieve a theoretical

66 *The urban village concept: the best examples are in Europe. The Pikku-Huopalanti project in Helsinki aims to create an extension to the housing in the city centre. Architects: Karii Piimies, Markku Lahti and Erkki Kantola.*

7 The motor car should be accommodated but not allowed to dominate the environment.

8 Ecologically sound forms of development and energy generation should be an integral part of the design to produce a sustainable human environment.

9 Full public involvement needs to be positive, genuine and creditable.

The idea is attractive because of the possibility of creating 'communities'. However, some form of public financial support would be necessary to provide the local employment opportunities, the shops, the schools, and above all to construct the rented housing that will be necessary to provide the social mix of people that is required to establish a community in the fullest sense. There are proposals for urban villages in a number of inner-city areas, but the concept is taking a long time to become reality. The best role models are in other European countries where high density urban living is more acceptable (Fig. 66).

1:1 ratio between jobs and residents able and willing to work.

4 The development should cater for changing social trends, including the increasing numbers of retired people and people working from home.

5 The mixture of uses should be accommodated with a variety of sizes and types of building. In the more densely built-up heart of the urban village, preference should be given on ground floors to shops, restaurants, pubs, workshops, studios and other active uses which bring life to the buildings and the spaces in front of them.

6 There should be a mixture of tenure both for housing and employment uses.

Housing improvement – Estate Action

A major problem in most inner-city areas relates to the difficult-to-let council housing estates, for which Estate Action was introduced in 1985 (Fig. 67). The concept is that finance is targeted to local authorities for the improvement of housing and its environment. This has usually been linked to the tenants becoming members of the area housing committee and participating in the decision-making process, including the spending of a local maintenance budget. In recent years Estate Action has also taken a more explicit role in economic regeneration and local employment creation.

Council housing which is likely to attract Estate Action funding usually

suffers from a complex mix of problems, combining physical decay with social and economic deprivation. Many estates are high-density and contain tower blocks and deck-access housing. The bids for government funding, which are made each year on the basis of competition between local authorities, have to demonstrate that all the possible options for the future development and management of the estate have been fully explored. The proposals are expected to find cost-effective solutions to key issues in the following areas:

1   Structure, design and layout: by providing physical improvements to the housing and environment.

2   Housing management: improvements through local management at estate and neighbourhood levels.

3   Tenant participation: by involving tenants in the regeneration and long-term management of their estate.

4   Choice and variety for tenants: by diversifying tenure and attracting private sector resources. Local authorities have to demonstrate on ability to attract other means of funding to bring about regeneration. This could be through the disposal of land and buildings, often at discounted rates, to allow housing associations and developers to provide low-cost housing for sale or for rent.

5   Social and economic problems: by establishing estate-based training and enterprise initiatives.

The key to the future of the estates is the restructuring of their layouts and pedestrian and vehicular access to the dwellings (Figs. 68 and 69). Measures in the past have included:

1   The demolition of tower blocks and their replacement with new low-rise

housing. In some cases maisonette blocks have been converted into houses by removing the top one or two storeys.

2   The removal of high-level walkways between deck-access blocks.

3   The construction of new roads and additional off-street car parking.

4   Environmental works, landscaping and the provision of private gardens.

The improvements to the dwellings have included:

1   Concrete repairs, external rendering and overcladding of tower and maisonette blocks to prevent water penetration and to increase the thermal performance.

2   The conversion of flat roofs to pitched roofs and the provision of insulation works, double-glazing and central heating.

3   The provision of entry-phones and security works, fire detectors, alarms and emergency lighting. Some schemes have reorganized the entrances and provided a

67 *Lea View, London, has been converted into highly popular housing by architects, Hunt Thompson Associates, who worked closely on the design proposals with the local residents.*

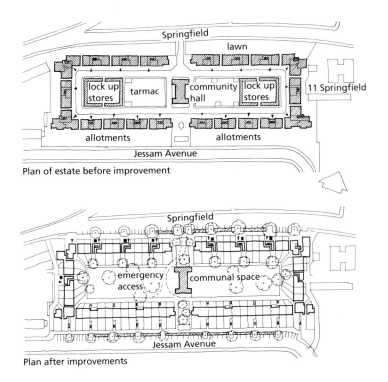

Springfield

lawn

lock up stores | tarmac | community hall | lock up stores | 11 Springfield

allotments | allotments

Jessam Avenue

Plan of estate before improvement

Springfield

emergency access | communal space

Jessam Avenue

Plan after improvements

Old plan, typical block | New plan

68 *Lea View, London: plans before and after improvement.*

69 *Castlevale HAT: division into neighbourhoods, restructuring in Area 7 and new housing in Area 6. Feasibility study by Department of Planning and Architecture, Birmingham City Council.*

The training is financed by the Enterprise Council, with some support from the Department of the Environment. Lewisham has also built child-care centres, so that single mothers can leave their children whilst working, and converted disused garages into workshops.

The Estate Action policy attempts to stabilize the community within estates. The plans endeavour to avoid saturating the estates with people with multiple problems, which may contribute to the rapid spiral of decline. It is hoped that this can be achieved through establishing balanced communities, with a stable nucleus of traditional family accommodation. Homelessness is being met in some instances by the provision of short-life tenancies following temporary improvement works.

The improvement of management is

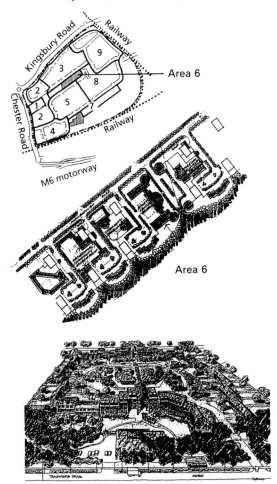

Kingsbury Road | Railway

Chester Road

M6 motorway

Area 6

Railway

Area 6

concierge system. In addition the ground floors of tower blocks are converted for community uses.

The provision of local estate offices is important. Some local authorities, such as the London Borough of Lewisham, have combined Estate Action with City Challenge and ERDF opportunities to maximize the potential for a multi-faceted approach to improvement (Fig. 70). They have developed schemes to bring people back into employment. A skills audit has been carried out on the estates with the intention that this could produce a pool of labour which can be employed on the improvement works. This has been supported by the training and organization of local people so that they can work on the Estate Action projects on a sub-contracting basis to the main contractors.

seen as a key objective. Localized management and maintenance is helping to achieve this but most significantly, the process has led to improvements in the approach by elected councillors and local authority officers. For the architects and planners, it has provided an opportunity for community design in real terms.

Housing Action Trusts

The concept of Housing Action Trusts (HATs) developed out of Estate Action. The difference is that the management of the housing passes to the Trust for the duration of the construction works (usually five years), after which it can pass to a housing association, a management co-operative or to the private sector, or it can pass back to the local authority if the tenants so wish. The HATs do not have planning powers, but they have responsibility for the economic and social improvement of their estates which are important if the physical improvements are to have long-term benefits. The measures adopted recognize the importance of initiatives being self-sustaining. They include:

1 Raising the general level of awareness of the community through educational means.

2 Anti-poverty action which recognizes that there will always be a problem of long-term unemployment. With this in mind help is given to enable people to more effectively utilize the limited financial and other resources available to them and to gain access to low-interest loans to purchase and replace essential household furniture and equipment.

3 Care and support to elderly people and single parents and young people, particularly children between the ages of 12 to 14 years of age who frequently cause vandalism and disturbance on the estates.

4 Training and education, particularly in self-assertiveness, neighbourhood skills, building construction, etc. Courses are directed so that the people can pass their knowledge on to others.

5 Improvements to raise the standard of health and leisure opportunities.

6 Women's issues, which includes helping to raise self-esteem.

7 The provision of managed workspace in which people can establish small businesses.

The North Hull Action Trust was the first HAT to be established in 1991. This has been followed by others at Waltham Forest in London, Liverpool, and at Castlevale in Birmingham (Fig. 69). In Hull the emphasis of the programme is the improvement of 2000 inter-war houses, combined with a small amount of selective new development, particularly for elderly people. In the other HATs the problems are more complex and the proposals

70 *Estate Action: environmental improvements at the Winslade Estate, London. Architects: Consultancy Services, Lewisham Housing.*

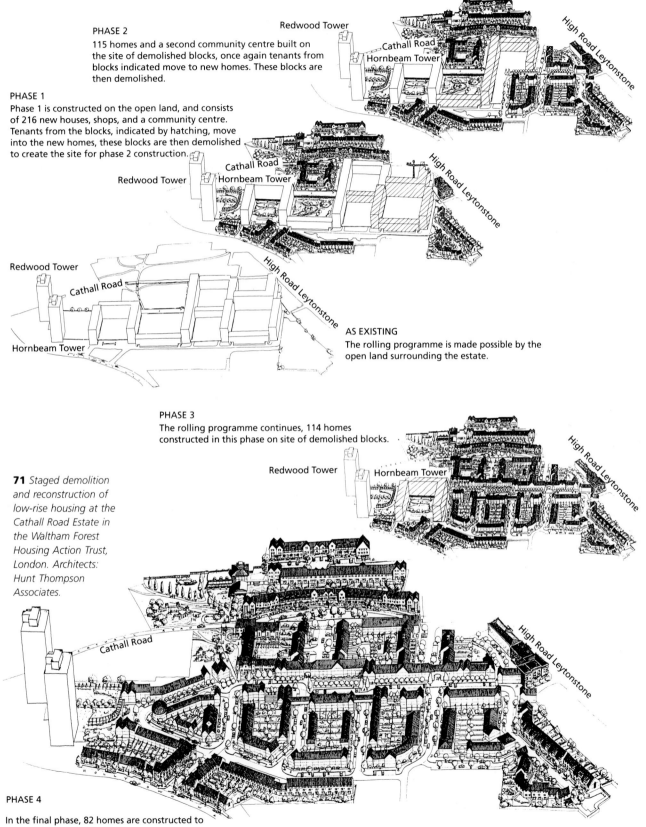

PHASE 2

115 homes and a second community centre built on the site of demolished blocks, once again tenants from blocks indicated move to new homes. These blocks are then demolished.

Redwood Tower

Cathall Road

Hornbeam Tower

High Road Leytonstone

PHASE 1

Phase 1 is constructed on the open land, and consists of 216 new houses, shops, and a community centre. Tenants from the blocks, indicated by hatching, move into the new homes, these blocks are then demolished to create the site for phase 2 construction.

Cathall Road

Redwood Tower

Hornbeam Tower

High Road Leytonstone

Redwood Tower

Cathall Road

High Road Leytonstone

Hornbeam Tower

AS EXISTING

The rolling programme is made possible by the open land surrounding the estate.

PHASE 3

The rolling programme continues, 114 homes constructed in this phase on site of demolished blocks.

Redwood Tower

Hornbeam Tower

High Road Leytonstone

71 Staged demolition and reconstruction of low-rise housing at the Cathall Road Estate in the Waltham Forest Housing Action Trust, London. Architects: Hunt Thompson Associates.

Cathall Road

High Road Leytonstone

PHASE 4

In the final phase, 82 homes are constructed to complete the redevelopment.

include some refurbishment of the existing
high-density flats and the construction of
new low-rise housing to replace existing
dwellings on a progressive basis (Fig. 71).

Private sector housing improvement

A major plank of urban regeneration in
most inner cities in the 1970s and early
1980s was the improvement of pre-1919
housing through the provision of
improvement grants to upgrade the
interiors, and the availability to local
authorities of the financial means to repair
the external fabric through enveloping.
There was also funding for environmental
improvement. The success of cities such as
Birmingham and Glasgow matches the
achievements of Baltimore, Rotterdam
and Bologna. Regrettably, improvement
grants are now subject to means testing
and enveloping has almost ceased in the
wake of continuing government cuts in
housing investment allocations to local
authorities.

This shortfall has not been met by the
private sector. There have been notable
successes by private developers who have
acquired empty local authority housing at
very low cost, and improved them for sale,
e.g. Minster Court in Liverpool by Barratt
Developments, but this contributes little
to meeting housing needs in the inner city.

Glasgow

Glasgow's rise in the last few years has
been dramatic. A remarkable Lord Provost
coined the phrase 'Glasgow smiles better'
(Glasgow's miles better) and the cheerful
slogan has helped to transform the city.
The city hosted the National Garden
Festival in 1988 and was recently
European City of Culture. It currently
projects itself as a major centre for
business services and tourism – a city of
European significance. The changes came

72 Templeton's factory,
Glasgow Green, which
was successfully
renovated as part of the
GEAR project.

about as a result of the action of many people and organizations. The most significant were the East End Project, the growth of tenant co-operatives, the regeneration of the Merchant City and Housing Improvement.

Glasgow East End Project – GEAR

Considerable assistance was given to Glasgow in the past by the Scottish Development Agency (SDA), which until its recent disbandment was a major instrument in Scotland for achieving urban regeneration. The GEAR project in the East End of Glasgow was its major responsibility.

Glasgow was perhaps the first city in Europe to experience the implications of post-industrial decline. In a very short space of time more than 20,000 jobs were lost as the great names of engineering crumbled in the 1960s (Fig. 73). The number of jobs lost in the subsidiary industries was equally devastating. This was accompanied by the largest slum clearance project in the world and the loss of population, from 145,000 (in 1951) to 45,000 in 1976. In total, the decline of the area presented a picture of urban devastation as bad as any in Europe. A pamphlet produced in 1988 by the Glasgow District Council puts it well: 'Throughout the East End industrial dereliction, endemic unemployment, worsening housing and health conditions plus low educational attainment were the norm. Everywhere dereliction and decay was apparent.'[12]

The project started in 1976 and its area covered 1600 hectares (4000 acres) of the city. The SDA's investment was financed by borrowing, within a limit set by the Scottish Office. The main task of the SDA was the co-ordination of the participants in GEAR. These and their responsibilities were as follows:[13]

1 Glasgow District Council – new housing, modernization, rehabilitation, other.

2 Strathclyde Regional Council – transport infrastructure, education, social services, community protection services.

3 Scottish Development Agency – land assembly/site preparation, factory building and business development, environmental works, recreation.

4 Scottish Special Housing Association – new housing, modernization, rehabilitation, other.

5 Housing Corporation – Local Housing Association, New Housing and rehabilitation.

6 Greater Glasgow Health Board – health issues.

7 Manpower Services Commission; Department of Health and Social Security job creation, training, etc.

8 Property Services Agency; the involvement of voluntary organizations under the urban programme.

The SDA organized a number of projects directly, most notably the refurbishment of the Templeton Business Centre (Fig. 72), and the Barras improvement. Templeton's, a deserted former carpet factory situated on the edge of Glasgow Green, has become a centre for launching and

New housing
Housing refurbishment
Open space provision
New employment
Strategic highway improvements
Programmed road improvements
Possible new road improvements or alignments

73 The Glasgow GEAR project: plan of development programme in 1980.

74 *'The Barras' provides a much needed low-cost shopping centre for the local community in the East End of Glasgow.*

supporting new enterprises – offering workshops, offices, shared services and equipment, loans and grants, and professional advice. The 'Barras' (Barrows) is a market of small shops, second-hand stalls and street traders. Close by, in what used to be a derelict area, small homes for owner-occupation have been built (Fig. 74).

The experience has many lessons for urban regeneration in the future. David Donnison and Alan Middleton analysed these in their book *Regenerating the Inner City: Glasgow's experience.*[14] Their overriding conclusions were as follows:

1 The effort to bring new sources of employment to the area has not brought any startling success, but since so many heads of households were elderly and not eligible for employment, good housing is much more important than job creation. The concern of most of the residents was to be rehoused within their own neighbourhood rather than be consigned to the peripheral estates.

2 The small factories built by the SDA would likely have been built anyway within the city. The economic benefits enjoyed by the GEAR area were probably won at the expense of other nearby areas.

3 With conventional small enterprise apparently unlikely to recruit from the

ranks of the long-term unemployed, other strategies which generate work and incomes for this group are desperately needed. The need is for community business, i.e. trading organizations owned and controlled by the local community, which aim to create jobs for local people, and retain and recycle any profits made for community purposes.

4 The priority of the GEAR project was modernization and improvement of housing which has been effective in upgrading the area but expensive.

5 The energy and collaboration evoked by public participation in housing should be extended into the planning and management of other local services.

6 There is much benefit to be gained from 'greening' the environment, but more thought needs to be given at the design stage to its maintenance.

Donnison and Middleton looked at the role of the SDA in urban regeneration in comparison with the UDCs in England and Wales. They considered that there are benefits from the extra powers which the UDCs have over those given to the SDA, but the lack of total power perhaps encouraged greater co-ordination between the participants.

The tenants' cooperatives
In the early 1980s, groups of Glasgow council tenants saw what was happening at Weller and Hesketh Streets in Liverpool (see p. 89). The opportunity came for them to take similar action when the government decided to slash Glasgow's Housing Investment Programme allocation for 1984–5 from £72 million to £49 million. The City Council responded by proposing to sell thousands of its houses to community ownership cooperatives. By 1987, the Council was employing a community worker with the remit to

76 *Housing improvement in the Castlemilk Estate, Glasgow.*

75 *Left: High-quality shops have been attracted to the revitalized Merchant City, Glasgow.*

encourage the tenants' movement and it had provided several tenants' halls and 'community flats' which could be used by a wide range of community groups, including tenants' associations. This provided the positive stimulus and now large numbers of local authority houses, in both the inner city and beyond, are managed by the tenants themselves. Some groups have built new housing whilst others have extended activities beyond housing renovation into job creation and improving the local economy. Some empty housing has been sold for homesteading.

The Merchant City

The old Merchant City is an eighteenth- and nineteenth-century quarter, originally the residences of Glasgow's tobacco lords, who lived above their work (Fig. 77). By the 1960s the area had become run-down, blighted by highway proposals and scheduled for comprehensive

redevelopment. Ten years later the buildings became more appreciated and subsequently were restored and converted into housing for middle-income people with the assistance of funding from the SDA. The Italian Centre is a fine example of what was achieved.[15] The developer, Douglas Loan, took a great financial risk and the success of the project shows the importance of local entrepreneurs in the regeneration process. His comment about the macro approach so often adopted in cities is highly relevant: 'When London developers came to take a look, their motivation was greed. But at the end of the day, what sort of city are you left with? There's nothing of quality' (Fig. 75).[16]

Housing improvement

A great deal of effort is now being concentrated on housing development within the inner city and beyond. There are proposals to redevelop the Gorbals including a large site at Crown Street. Significant work is also currently being undertaken by Chris Purslow and the City Council's Department of Architecture and Related Services in estates such as Castlemilk on the edge of the inner city. The strategy for the estate of 5000 dwellings was developed by the Castlemilk Partnership which was formed in 1988 after the publication of the government's 'New Life for Scotland' report. The Management Committee for the project is chaired by the Scottish Office and includes representatives of the local community, the City Council, the Glasgow Development Agency, Scottish Housing, the Training Agency, the Employment Service and – representing the private sector – Glasgow Opportunities. Amongst its major objectives are the following priorities: to arrest the population decline and stabilize the community; to increase local economic activity; to provide a quantity of types of housing and tenure with a mixture of refurbishment of existing housing and the construction of new housing on cleared sites; to develop a high quality of social, health, education and community care; to promote environmental improvement. To date, the work to the existing housing has been of a very high standard. Only time will tell how successful the social and economic strategy will be (Figs. 78 and 79).

Birmingham

City Centre development
During the late 1970s and the 1980s, the traditional economic base of the city of Birmingham, built on the metal-working industries, went into serious decline. In the mid-1980s the City Council took a series of key decisions to promote positive city-centre change as an important part of the economic revival of the city as a whole. The construction of an International Convention Centre was

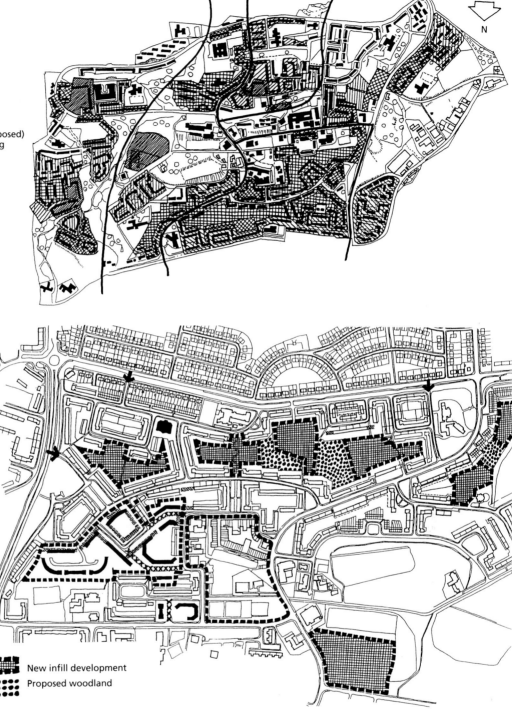

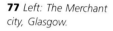

High quality council
housing (existing or proposed)
Council housing requiring
investment
Community ownership
Home ownership
Scottish homes
Mixed tenure

77 *Left: The Merchant
city, Glasgow.*

79 *Regeneration
strategy for the
Castlemilk estate,
Glasgow.*

New infill development
Proposed woodland

conceived as a 'business tourism' flagship
project, acting both to stimulate the
service sector in the city centre and to
provide a combination of business and
cultural facilities, including a major new
concert hall (Fig. 80). The substantial
environmental improvements in the city
centre included the construction of
Centenary Square and Centenary Way, the
downgrading and remodelling of the inner
ring road into a ground level boulevard
system with surface crossings for

pedestrians; and at Victoria Square, a
premier public space of great proportion
has been designed by Rory Coonan (Arts
Council), Dhruva Mistry (sculptures),
Bettina Furnée (letter carver) and others
(Fig. 81). In carrying out these works, the
City Council has declared its intention – to
create an environment commensurate with
a European city of significance such as
Barcelona, Lyon and Rotterdam – which it
sees as essential to secure its future
economic prosperity.

78 *Left: New life for
difficult-to-let flats in
the Castlemilk estate,
Glasgow.*

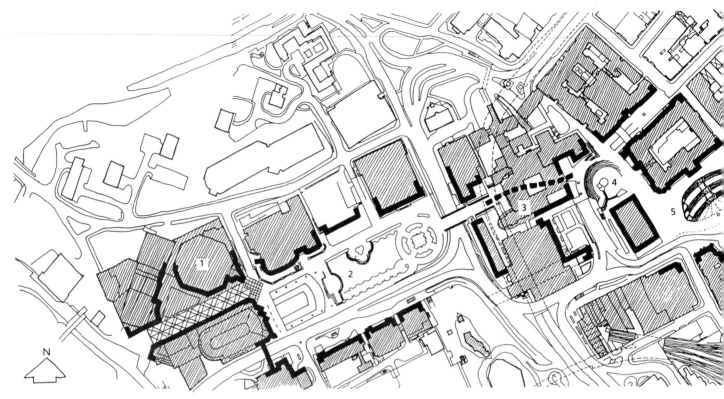

1 Conference centre
2 Centenary Square
3 City library
4 Chamberlan Square
5 Victoria Square

80 *Plan of Centenary Square and city centre spaces, Birmingham.*

The 'Quarters'

The City Council's strategy also highlighted seven areas or 'Quarters', each based on past and present economic and physical roles (Fig. 81). The strategy sought to reinforce the individuality of each Quarter by encouraging appropriate land uses and enhancing physical environment. The famous Jewellery Quarter is one such area where considerable refurbishment has taken place over recent years (Fig. 83).

Housing

Housing has always been a key part of Birmingham's urban renewal strategy. During the 1970s and 1980s the city established a reputation for urban renewal from the large 'enveloping' programmes in its pre-1914 bylaw streets. In the Birmingham Heartlands project the City

1 Gunsmiths
2 Aston Triangle
3 Jewellery
4 City Centre
5 Greater Convention Centre Area
6 Warwick Bar / Digbeth
7 Chinese Quarter and Markets Area

81 *The Birmingham 'Quarters'.*

82 *The new Victoria Square, Birmingham.*

83 *The Jewellery Quarter.*

Council has formed a development agency with a group of major construction companies to regenerate a large tract of derelict land four miles from the city centre. The Castlevale Estate, built in the 1960s, is to become a Housing Action Trust, in which many of the high-rise blocks are to be replaced on an incremental basis with two-storey houses.

Liverpool

Waterfront regeneration
The symbol of urban regeneration in Liverpool is the restoration of the Albert Dock and Warehouses which form the largest group of Grade 1 listed buildings in Britain (Fig. 84). The Merseyside Development Corporation has made this their flagship for urban regeneration of the

84 *Left: The Albert Dock, Liverpool.*

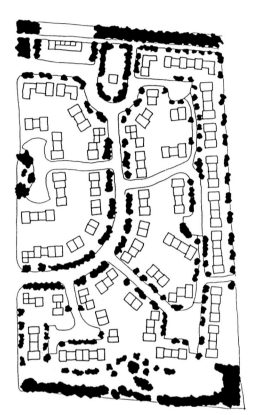

85 *The Eldonian Village. Architects: The Wilkinson Hindle Halsall Lloyd Partnership.*

river frontage. Part of the Tate Gallery has come north and the former Dock Traffic Office has been converted into the Granada TV News Centre. Other buildings and spaces to benefit from refurbishment are St George's Hall in the centre of the city, and the Pierhead. The city was successful in the 1993 round of City Challenge bids to tackle the problems of one of the most deprived inner cities from the riverside up to the two Cathedrals and the University. Some of the work in this area has already been initiated through the local churches. Derrick Walters, the Dean of the Anglican Cathedral, has been instrumental in establishing a charitable Cathedral company, which is now the power behind one of Britain's largest inner-city redevelopments called 'Project Rosemary'. By levering cash from the Government, working with private developers, and persuading the city council to give the company 'preferred development status', an outlay of £60m has come from public and private sources. This has produced

250 new houses, a hospital and an estimated saving and/or creation of 2000 jobs in servicing, manufacturing and construction.[17] The city is also to benefit from a massive injection of EC funding between 1993 and 1999.

Cooperative housing

A most important lesson to come from Liverpool relates to the growth of cooperative housing in the inner city. The movement began in the early 1970s as a management buy-out from private landlords who were unwilling or unable to rehabilitate the houses they owned. From this came the new-build projects at Weller and Hesketh Streets and the Eldonian Village. From 1978, over 2000 new homes have been provided in Liverpool through the cooperative renewal projects.

The Eldonian Community Association was formed in 1984 with the primary objective of re-housing its members (145 families) from an area of slum housing and poor environment, in a way that would keep the community together. Following the closure of the Tate and Lyle sugar refinery, the owners of the site, English Estates, were so impressed with the Eldonians' proposals for community use that they offered the land to them. The City Council opposed the scheme on grounds that cooperatives were 'elitist, exclusive and discriminatory and that public funds should be channelled towards the provision of council-owned housing on the basis of proven housing need'.[18] With direct support from Michael Heseltine, the Secretary of State for the Environment, the scheme proceeded in 1987 (Fig. 85). The Eldonians have now moved on beyond their initial housing objectives into the wider field of urban regeneration. They have established a commercial garden centre as an employment generation project, developed other forms of skill training to help people find work, and converted an old warehouse into a sports centre.[19]

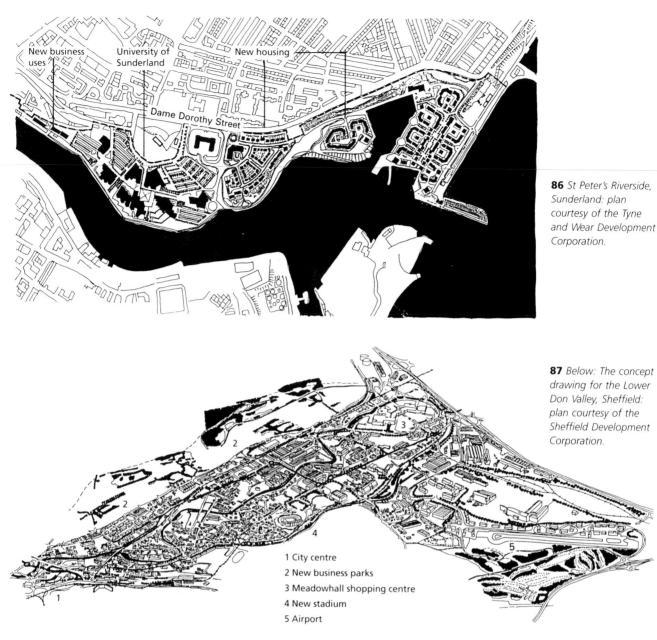

86 *St Peter's Riverside, Sunderland: plan courtesy of the Tyne and Wear Development Corporation.*

87 *Below: The concept drawing for the Lower Don Valley, Sheffield: plan courtesy of the Sheffield Development Corporation.*

1 City centre
2 New business parks
3 Meadowhall shopping centre
4 New stadium
5 Airport

Tyne and Wear

The final loss of shipbuilding on the Tyne and Wear rivers in 1993, together with the demise of the coal industry, is perhaps the most symbolic illustration of the de-industrialization process that is taking place in Britain. New industries are being attracted to Tyneside and Wearside by the Development Corporation and the local authorities, but few of the new factories, such as those in the Business Park overlooking the Wear, will employ many people (Fig. 86). This problem is recognized by Alistair Balls, the Development Corporation's Chief Executive who, in a recent article on urban regeneration in *The Planner*, commented that 'experience seems to suggest that "trickle-down" does not work unless there is a specific targeting of public resources

and benefits to the most disadvantaged population groups, a lot of time spent, and sensible collaborative processes between the various administrative structures. The "top-down" must always be complemented by the "bottom-up" approach'.[20] It is to be hoped that Balls's foresight can be put into action, for the banks of the Rivers Tyne and Wear are now characterized not with the cranes of the shipyards but the greening from the environmental improvement schemes.

Sheffield

The early 1980s saw a rapid decline in Sheffield's steel and heavy engineering industry, resulting in the loss of over 25,000 jobs in the industry, and leaving one-third of the lower Don Valley disused.

88 *Above right: The Don Valley Stadium, Sheffield. Architects: DBS Architects, Sheffield.*

89 *Right: Sheffield Business Park. Architects: HLM Architects.*

The problems demanded a radical approach. As in the former USA steel city of Pittsburgh, a strong bond was formed between the City Council and the business community to work in partnership to approach economic and urban regeneration in a positive manner. In 1984 came the realization that to rescue the remainder of the steel industry, new industries such as information technology, precision engineering services, tourism and cultural industries needed to be attracted. The plans were also underpinned by a belief in the importance of leisure in modern city life.

The catalyst for the approach was the successful bid to host the World Student Games in 1991. The centre of the city was given a considerable uplift with the construction of the International Sports Centre, the refurbishment of the Lyceum Theatre, and of the bus and railway stations: in addition part of the Hyde Park flats which stand on the hill above the railway station were enveloped and converted, by one of the city's housing associations, initially into accommodation for the games' competitors but thereafter to provide permanent homes for young people in the city.

The area designated for most of the sports buildings was the Lower Don Valley (Fig. 87). The East End Park, Sheffield and Tinsley Canal Corridor and other 'greening' projects were undertaken as a means of regenerating the area as a whole and supporting existing industry by making the area more attractive to a new range of companies. The largest of the city council's projects for the student games was the 25,000-seater Don Valley Stadium (Fig. 89). Located nearby is the Don Valley Arena, a multi-purpose indoor sports and leisure building. The Sheffield Development Corporation has recently added to this with the development of a number of business parks (Fig. 88). One of the two routes of the Sheffield supertram runs through the Don Valley to

the Meadowhall out-of-town shopping centre, completed in 1990. This is a massive development, which rivals the Metro Centre in Gateshead as the largest in Britain. However, its impact on the centres of the towns and cities within the Yorkshire and Humberside Region and beyond is considerable.

The level of public investment by the City Council for the Don Valley projects built between 1985 and 1991 was enormous. Some of the funding came from the government's urban programme and from the European Regional Development Fund but much came from the city's own resources, i.e. borrowed money which the city is now having to repay. The project caused great concern in government

90 *Salford Quays, Manchester.*

circles, but in its own way Sheffield's vision of using sport as a means to achieve urban regeneration is comparable to that of Barcelona's and equally worthy for the financial support that Manchester's bid for the Olympic Games in 2000 would have received from the government, had it been successful.[21]

Manchester

Manchester will be an important focus of urban regeneration in the future. A new tramway is operating in the city centre and two urban development corporations have been established – Central Manchester and Trafford. Salford Quays (Fig. 90) is a flagship project for the area. Alongside the canals, which were once the veins of the Industrial Revolution, converted warehouses and new houses, flats and apartments are proving popular. There is also a new student village comprising over 1000 housing units. But beyond the glitter of the city centre and the new projects by the development corporations there are areas of great deprivation. Hulme is one of these areas.

Hulme

Hulme was once an area of densely-packed streets just on the edge of the city centre. During the 1960s the area was comprehensively redeveloped with system-built crescents. Within five years the families for whom the deck access maisonettes had been designed were moved out and the crescents became single person and all-adult housing. Despite the establishment of a vibrant, alternative-lifestyle community, deteriorating physical and social conditions have led to the need for wholesale demolition. Manchester City Council and its partner in the project, AMEC Plc, has set up a City Challenge joint venture company, Hulme Regeneration Ltd, to prepare and manage the regeneration strategy. An intensive

programme of workshops and Planning for Real exercises has clearly indicated that the preference of the residents is firstly for low-rise development following the pattern of the former streets, and secondly for the construction of a major new park. There is also a desire for some medium-rise housing of four and five storeys to reflect an urban character. The participants want to see 'streets that go places, streets that connect'; they wanted the development to be 'an essential and integrated part of Manchester'.[22]

Leeds

Leeds is now competing with Manchester, Liverpool and others to become the commercial capital of the north of England. To do so, it has made a considerable effort to upgrade the city centre and many of its fine Victorian buildings (Fig. 91). The Corn Exchange has been converted into a speciality shopping centre; the arcades and the covered market have been refurbished and the City Art Gallery has been given a most impressive facelift by Jeremy Dixon and the City Council's in-house architects. The Leeds Development Corporation has most successfully pursued the improvement of the run-down River Aire industrial waterfront with a mixture of new housing and refurbished warehouses. There is undoubtedly an air of confidence in the city which should assist its economic and physical recovery.[23]

Hull

The City of Kingston upon Hull (population 250,000) suffered from the complete loss in the 1970s of its fishing industry and the movement downstream of its former dock-related activities. Most of the nineteenth-century docks in the city centre have been refurbished with funding from the Derelict Land Grant and both the Urban Programme and the European Regional Development Fund (Fig. 92).

92 *The regeneration of the city-centre docks, Hull.*

93 *Self-help by young homeless people and Giroscope, Hull.*

91 *Left: The recently refurbished Victoria Arcade, Leeds.*

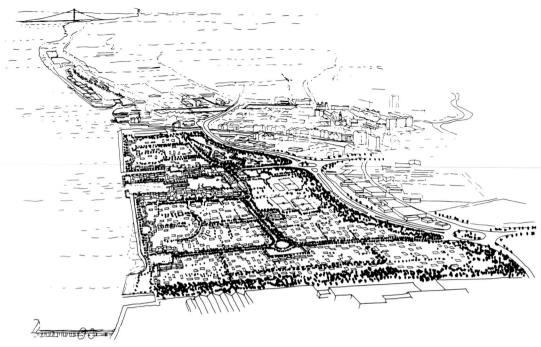

94 *Victoria Dock, Hull: drawing by the author when City Architect.*

The principal works have been the refurbishment of old warehouses, the construction of new housing and offices and environmental improvements. At Victoria Dock, a major private housing developer, Bellway Homes (Urban Renewal), has been working in partnership with the city council to redevelop a large derelict site with over 1000 private and social houses (Fig. 94). In 1987, Bellway Homes received a £17 million City Grant from the government to prepare the site for the development. This included funding for over a mile of new river walls and promenades, which gave the city extensive access to the River Humber frontage for the first time in 200 years.

A completely opposite, but no less significant, project in Hull is the improvement of pre-1919 inner-city housing at Wellsted Street into homes for young people by the Giroscope workers cooperative. The cooperative benefited from low-interest loans and charitable donations: also the young people were prepared to carry out the building work themselves for payment equivalent only to unemployment benefit. The cooperative was founded in 1985 when a group of young people managed to raise £7000 to buy a small run-down house. When improved, this house was rented to other young people and another two houses were purchased. This way the cooperative gathered both momentum and building skills. It now has several houses in the area and has developed a food club, a printing press and is helping to establish a further, but independent, housing cooperative (Fig. 93).

Swansea

The revitalization of the city centre, the Lower Swansea Valley, and the former docks and the seafront, was the cornerstone of Swansea's programme of urban regeneration, which followed fundamental changes in the local economy in the 1950s and 1960s. The programme included the expansion of the central shopping area, the provision of new recreational and sports facilities, the planting of millions of trees to form new woodland and the construction of new housing around the former docks in the Maritime Village. Key to the commercial revival was the designation of an enterprise zone which has attracted substantial amounts of new business.

The importance of the Swansea development is that the city was the first industrial seaport in the UK to set about its problems in a comprehensive manner. Moreover, its significant achievement has come about without the presence of an urban development corporation or any other form of direct government intervention. The success came entirely from public initiative. The city managed to exploit the possibility of every form of public finance and actively sought partnership arrangements with the private sector wherever possible. Maximum benefit was gained from South Wales's special economic status with respect to

95 *Right: Maritime Village, Swansea.*

government aid. The process of implementing the development was simplified considerably by the fact that most of the land was publicly owned. This made it possible for the City Council, as coordinators, to have control over the overall planning and phasing of the various developments and infrastructure construction.

The first buildings, the new leisure centre and 54 local authority housing units, were completed in 1975. The Marina was completed in 1982, after which a profusion of private sector developments followed. The Village now possesses a conference hotel, a food store, offices, shops, restaurants, an art gallery, a hostel, a boatclub, a public house and a multi-storey car park (Fig. 95). The form of development has brought about the creation of some fine urban townscape and architecture. In recent years the City Council has allocated funds for architectural enhancements. From this, contributions were made to special detailing, and for the inclusion of statues, sculptures and historical reference points in the new spaces.

Urban design was important in the planning process as Trevor Osborne, the

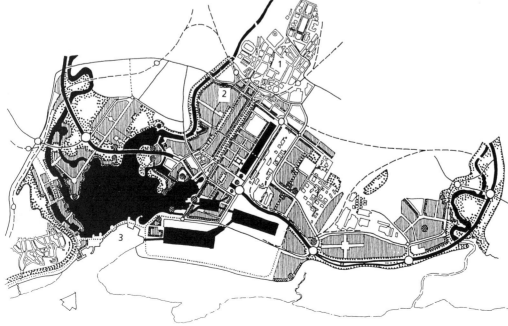

Main landscape features

Development areas

Wetland habitat

Key building frontages

1 City centre

2 Butetown

3 Barrage

96 *Cardiff Bay Strategy Plan. Reproduced by courtesy of Cardiff Bay Development Corporation.*

97 *Private housing development at Penarth.*

City's Chief Architect and Planning Officer at the time of the development explains: 'It is time to restate the key role town planning has in identifying potentials and their interrelationships, and in formulating frameworks for the skills of the architect designers, engineers and land managers to realise those opportunities and for creating a climate of confidence and direction for investment by all sectors of the market'.[24] Swansea is an example for all cities to follow.

Cardiff

The city of Cardiff has enormous potential in the future as a 'European Capital City'. Its revitalization is currently centred on

the regeneration of the former docks and industrial land around Cardiff Bay. Established in 1987, the Cardiff Bay Development Corporation commissioned Llewelyn-Davies Planning to produce an overall urban design concept. This endeavours to create a sense of place for the development as a whole through the blending of new development with the improvement of the best of the old environment and buildings. The setting for this, around the bay, is quite unique.

The key to the regeneration proposals is the construction of a barrage across the entrance to the bay to create a freshwater lake (Fig. 96). The proposals received considerable opposition from conservationists who were concerned about the impact of the proposals on the existing marine life.

The proposals also include the construction of 6000 new houses and the refurbishment of 2000 existing dwellings in the Bay area. A substantial proportion of the 25 per cent social housing is meeting special needs in existing communities. Housing for single people and sheltered housing for elderly people is being produced through partnership arrangements with housing associations. The plan also provides for the construction of two million sq. ft (200,000 sq. m.) of new office space. The existing industries in the Bay will be protected and nurtured with industrial improvement area policies, which will upgrade vehicular access, services and the environment. There will be a wide range of public buildings including four new primary schools and increased nursery facilities, surgeries, a family centre, an elderly persons' support unit, and extensive leisure and tourism facilities. Amongst these are a Maritime Centre, a centre for the performing arts and a 'Sky Tower' which will combine housing with a number of commercial and leisure uses. The jewel in the crown is the new Welsh National Opera House.

The first works to be completed have been centred on the road construction programme to open up sites for development. The first housing development is at Atlantic Quays, where a number of extremely fine nineteenth-century warehouses have been superbly refurbished. Butetown, which used to be the commercial centre to the former industries in the area, is being extensively refurbished and given a new lease of life. The development corporation has also funded the renovation of the seaside promenade and pier at Penarth and secured an impressive development of private housing around a marina at the headland beyond (Fig. 97).

London

London comprises one-eighth of Britain's population. It is managed through 33 separate Boroughs and there is no overall elected body to address the huge strategic issues within a city of great contrasts. It possesses two of the richest Boroughs in the country, the City of London and the City of Westminster, and 10 of the poorest such as Hackney, Southwark and Lambeth where the social deprivation dwarfs anything that exists in other comparable areas of the country. Between 1961 and 1986, the outward drift of the population from inner London was in the region of 500,000 people.[25] The movement of population was not only to the outer metropolitan areas such as Reading and Southend, but further afield to Wiltshire, Oxfordshire, Northamptonshire, Cambridgeshire and Suffolk. The Office of Population Censuses and Surveys predicts that this trend will continue until the end of the century and that an additional 1.3 million people will move to these areas. This movement of population is shadowed by the exodus of industry and jobs.

There are a number of developments that could in the future have a considerable impact on London: the development of King's Cross, the Channel Tunnel route, the redevelopment around St Paul's Cathedral, to name but a few. None, however, are on the scale of – or of such national significance – as the development of London's Docklands.

London Docklands

Purpose
The redevelopment of the London Docklands is the most significant urban regeneration project which the government has stimulated since 1979. The designated area of the Urban Development Corporation is some 8.5 square miles with

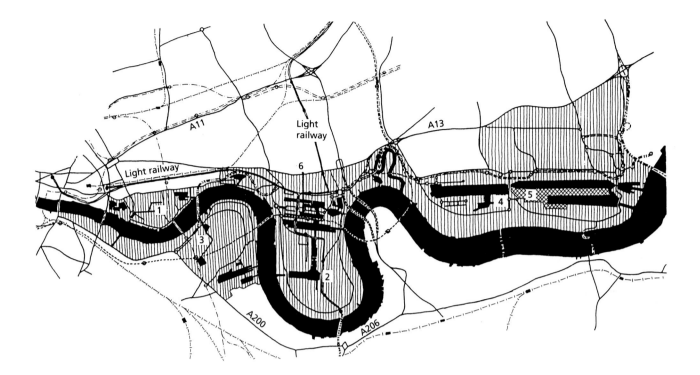

98 *Overall plan of the London Docklands development. Plan by courtesy of London Docklands Development Corporation.*

5000 acres (2000 hectares) of land, the largest single project of its kind in the world (Figs. 98 and 99).

The London Docklands Development Corporation (LDDC) was founded in 1981. It is controlled by a Board of 13 members, each appointed by the Secretary of State for the Environment. There are around 80 staff appointed to manage the urban regeneration process but most of the planning and project work is undertaken by outside consultants. There is an in-house team of landscape architects which, over the years, has carried out some excellent work. The LDDC is the planning authority but – unlike its predecessors, the new town development corporations – it is not a direct provider of housing. It has responsibility to acquire and prepare land for development, and to provide the infrastructure of roads, a light railway, fibre-optic mail and a small airport. Between 1981–91 the LDDC spent over £1.3 billion of public money which attracted £9.1 billion of private sector finance.[26]

Employment

By 1981, employment in port-related activities, which in the 1950s was 30,000,

had plummeted to 2000.[27] The Development Corporation's forecast is that 200,000 new jobs will be created by 2001 within the designated area.[28] Between 1981 and 1991 there was an increase in employment by some 26,000.[29] Only 2000 of these went to people living in the three London Boroughs. Most of the increases were in the service section, whilst jobs in production actually decreased.[30]

Housing

Some 15,000 new houses were built between 1981 and 1993, of which around 2000 were housing association-rented or shared-ownership. Almost all of the new housing was priced far beyond the reach of the local people. The prices reflected the huge increase in land values which rose from less than £100,000 per acre in 1980 to £1 million or more per acre in 1984. At the same time, the housing investment programmes of the three dockland boroughs – Newham, Southwark and Tower Hamlets – had been reduced in real terms by 50 per cent.[31] However, the policy has raised the proportion of public to private sector housing to near-equal from a situation in 1981 where the public sector was the dominant tenure.

99 *The London Docks and the Canary Wharf development seen from Greenwich.*

100 *St Catherine's Dock, London.*

101 *Right: Tobacco Dock, London Docklands.*

Transport

The inadequacies, in the early years of the life of the LDDC, of a market-led transport policy which did not relate to land-use planning is one of the most evident faults with the development so far. The Docklands Light Railway was the most significant aspect of the LDDC's policy, in its early years, for providing local access roads and transport projects to stimulate private development. For this reason, it was routed through the centre of the Isle of Dogs whilst the people live around the outside. This meant that it offered no benefit to most of the community. At peak times the capacity is more than exceeded and improvements are in hand. At weekends it does not run at all. The long-promised extension to London Underground's Jubilee Line was delayed, whilst vast sums were spent on networks of roads to serve the new developments.

Relationship with the local community

Until 1987, relationships with the three London Boroughs and with the local population were very poor. The LDDC worked in isolation and it generally seemed to the local people who lived within the designated area that the LDDC was not there for their benefit. Some improvement fortunately came about in the mid-1980s, after the occupation by local residents of sites proposed for private housing development. This led to the construction of rented housing at Cherry Garden Pier and Swan Road in Rotherhithe. This was followed by other campaigns by the local community – notably against the Canary Wharf development, the new six-lane road at South Poplar and the LDDC's proposals for the Royal Docks which culminated in the preparation by the local community of the 'People's Plan'. By 1987, public perception of the LDDC had become so negative that it was seriously affecting the

development process. The lack of infrastructure and community facilities also added to the problems. To counter this, the LDDC adopted a new approach with the three local authorities which, by this time, were beginning to recognize the inevitability of public/private sector partnerships. 'Agreements' or 'Accords' were signed in which the LDDC revised its objectives in order to 'secure the lasting physical, economic and social regeneration of the UDA'.[32]

This was accompanied by a more community-minded approach on the part of the LDDC – which has also been reflected in the policies of the second-round Urban Development Corporations in other cities. The new approach has been followed by the provision of social housing (such as Windsor Park) – but funded by housing associations rather than the local authorities. A Community Services Division (CSD) within the Development Corporation has also been established, with responsibility for social housing, joint planning, education and training, and community development. The CSD was given a number of objectives: that local people secure advantage from regeneration; that balanced communities were fostered; that services were delivered

102 *Shadwell Basin, London Docklands. Architects: MacCormac Jamieson Prichard.*

to meet the needs of those who live, work and employ in the UDA, and that decent housing is provided at a price which local people can afford to buy or rent.[33] A major breakthrough was the provision from 1989 of grants to community groups, funding for childcare/equal opportunities and community employment projects, housing and employment. Employment and training opportunities are built into planning gain agreements and an East London Compact, modelled on the Boston Compact in the USA, has been set up between schools and employers. One of the TECS, part of government policy to encourage private sector funding of training provision, has been sponsored by an East London company. However, there is no direct intervention in the local economy and the primary emphasis is still on speculative development, with the emphasis on the market-oriented approach.

The four management areas

The management of Docklands is divided into four areas: Wapping, Isle of Dogs, Surrey Docks, and the Royal Docks. These make a convenient basis for briefly describing the most significant developments.

Wapping

The LDDC's first project was the conversion of St Catherine's Dock, close to the Tower of London (Fig. 100), into a major tourist destination. The overall impression of that development is good. There is an interesting mix of restored warehouses and walkways around the old basins, new office buildings and the Tower Hotel. Across the river can be seen the massive Butler's Wharf project, into which modern elements have been skilfully integrated into the converted warehouses. Next to this is the new Design Museum.

Wapping High Street is one of the most handsome and evocative places in all of Docklands. Typical is the Gun House at Gun Wharves, a faithful restoration into luxury flats. Rugged nineteenth-century warehouses line the river side of the street, where they were originally placed to serve the ships tied up alongside. To the north of Wapping High Street is an area of new housing, following the newly-constructed canal bounded on one side by the walls of the former London Dock, in which some of the houses sit. Here there is a variety of houses designed by different architects in a style 'reminiscent of Amsterdam'.[34] The canal leads to Tobacco Dock. Built in 1811 as a tobacco warehouse with rum vaults below, the Grade 1 listed building has been converted successfully by the Terry Farrell Partnership into a shopping centre on the American 'festival market' model, with a mixture of tourist shops and cafes. However, unlike most of its American counterparts, it appears to be struggling to survive (Fig. 101). The new housing at Shadwell Basin by former RIBA president Richard MacCormac is striking. Further to the east is Narrow Street, which like parts of Wapping High Street is dramatically attractive in places (Fig. 102).

Isle of Dogs

Most of the land around the Millwall and West India Docks, including Canary Wharf, were included in the 425 acres

(170 hectares) Isle of Dogs Enterprise
Zone (EZ). The Isle of Dogs is now
dominated by the Canary Wharf
development, which was expected by the
Development Corporation to create 50,000
jobs. The 12 million sq. ft (1.15 million
sq. m.) office project by the now-bankrupt
American developers, Olympia and York,
took full advantage of the enterprise zone
opportunities. It has been estimated that
the cost to the public purse of these
subsidies is about £1.33 billion, assuming
construction costs of £4 billion and
corporation tax at 33 per cent.[35] Cesar
Pelli's tower is tall – 800 feet or the
equivalent of 80 storeys – which dominates
the skyline from neighbouring parts of
London. But it is not the height that is the
problem when looked at close-up, but scale
and density of the development in relation
to the amount of land in the area that is
undeveloped. Instead of a lively mix of uses
and activities – with real neighbourhoods
such as those that exist in many other parts
of London – the single use development
lacks life at the weekend. It also has no
relationship to the surrounding residential
neighbourhoods, either in social and
economic terms or as the provider of
employment opportunities.

Most of the other commercial buildings
do little to improve the overall impression
of the new development in the Isle of
Dogs. A small number of buildings do,
however, have considerable individual
merit. Heron Quays, designed by Nicholas
Lacey, was the first scheme to respond
intimately to the water-embracing areas of
the Docks within it. Later buildings
include the Financial Times printing
works by Nicholas Grimshaw and Partners
(close to the approach to the Blackwell
Tunnel), the Reuters building, designed
by Richard Rogers, and – perhaps the
most outstanding structure on the entire
Isle of Dogs – the whimsical water-
pumping station by John Outram. There
are many smart flats overlooking the
Thames, including the renowned Cascades

103 *Shad Thames, one
of the finest streets in
London's Docklands.*

by architects CZWG, but the best by far is Jeremy Dixon's Compass Point, complete with its trellises along the river walk.[36]

Surrey Docks

Surrey Docks extends along the south side of the Thames from London Bridge to Bermondsey and Rotherhithe in the east. It contains perhaps the finest street in Docklands – Shad Thames (Fig. 103). The stretch of waterfront development from London Bridge to Tower Bridge and on to Shad Thames contains a mixture of refurbished buildings and new infill development (Fig. 105) which avoids the pastiche feeling so evident elsewhere in Docklands. There are a number of extremely good examples of the 'blending'[37] of new with old buildings – the Hay's Galleria (Fig. 104), the new Design Museum, the Clove building in Shad Thames and China Wharf. Prince Charles illustrates his book *Urban Villages* with New Concordia Wharf, a restored warehouse complex providing flats, offices and studio workspace.[38] Brian Edwards, in his book *London Docklands*, praises the planning and design approach in this part of Docklands: 'The willingness with which developers have created urban spaces in this area of Docklands should dispel the myth that planning authorities are the principal means of creating amenities. Here, in this relatively deregulated part of London, a mixture of enterprising developers and architects aware of the urban dimension (as against simply the building dimension) has formed some attractive new squares out of a derelict jigsaw of dilapidated warehouses'.[39]

Greenland Dock was the subject of a master-plan by Conran Roche in 1984 which represented an unusual approach to planning at that time by the Development Corporation (Fig. 106). This established a height limit of four storeys which has generally been adhered to, except in the mixed development of flats, studios, offices

and shops at Baltic Quays which overlooks the South Dock Marina. The result of the plan is that the development has a European feel. Greenland Passage, by Danish architects Kjaer and Richter, in fact owes its design forms to much of the early IBA work in Berlin.

The Surrey Docks area also includes a swathe of riverside developments in Rotherhithe. One of the best housing schemes is at Woolfe Crescent, which overlooks the newly-created Albion Channel. Brian Edwards rightly observes that this part of the London Docklands development has succeeded in architectural and urban design terms. He considers it very English. 'The impression from Stave Hill is one of pleasant greenery with brick cottages clustered into village-like groups . . . the lack of deliberate ordering and the love of mixed landscape and urban design are the quintessence of Englishness. Docklands may be the international market place of the LDDC, but from Surrey Docks it remains indelibly English in spirit'.[40]

The Royal Docks

The greatest design challenge of all remains the Royal Docks, which form the largest remaining city development site in Europe. To date there has been a considerable investment in roads, but the only completed development is the London City airport. The approach that is now being considered is the construction of inner-city 'urban-villages'. These will be more low-key than previous developments in Docklands and will include affordable homes for sale and housing for rent 'to improve the tenure mix'. It is now recognized that small-scale community development designed with recognizable high streets, churches and schools is most likely to succeed.[41] The plans also include a 23,000-seat sports stadium and an arts centre.

Like the new towns of the 1960s in their time, the development in the London

104 *Hay's Galleria, Rotherhithe, London Docklands.*

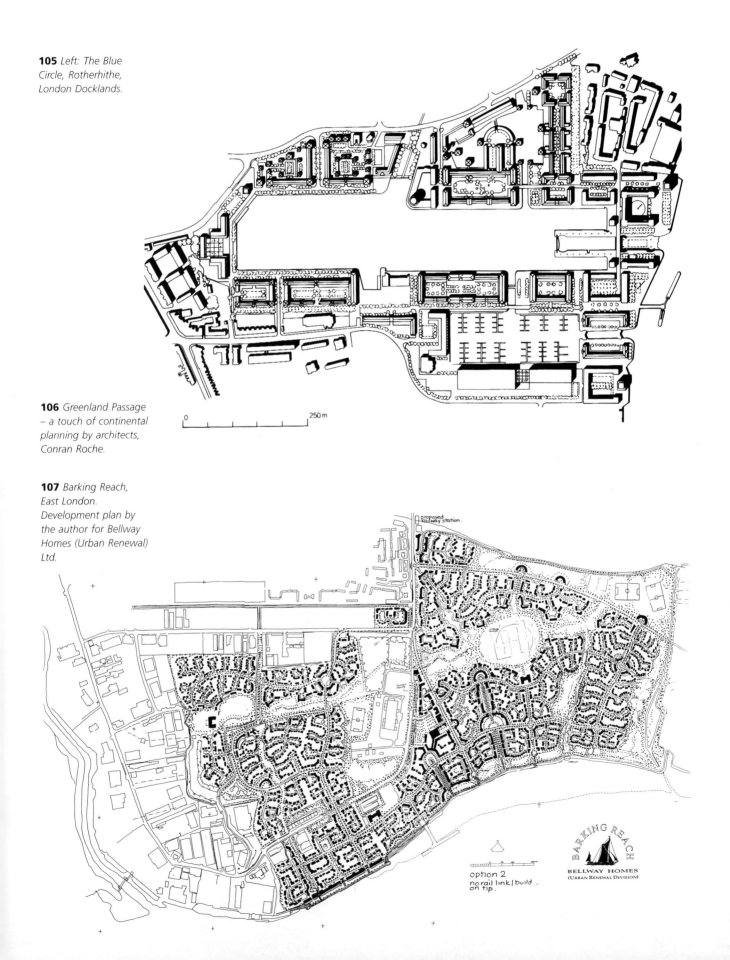

105 *Left: The Blue Circle, Rotherhithe, London Docklands.*

106 *Greenland Passage – a touch of continental planning by architects, Conran Roche.*

0   250 m

107 *Barking Reach, East London. Development plan by the author for Bellway Homes (Urban Renewal) Ltd.*

option 2
no rail link/build
on tip.

BARKING REACH

BELLWAY HOMES
(URBAN RENEWAL DIVISION)

Docklands has been subject to much criticism. Some is justified, particularly the limited social objectives and the over-development at Canary Wharf. However, there is much to praise. In some areas there are substantial amounts of ordinary family housing with children playing in the streets and schools nearby. This is succeeding in bringing back into the city many people who would otherwise move out to the suburbs and beyond, and surely worth the effort.

East Thames corridor

After several years of speculation, Michael Howard, the Secretary of State for the Environment, finally, at the end of March 1993, announced plans to establish a Task Force to co-ordinate the extension of the Docklands model to the Lower Thames. This included a £4.5 billion package of transport projects, including the Jubilee Line extension. The aims of the plan are to build by the year 2015 between 60,000–128,000 new homes, 4–10 million sq. m. (43–100 million sq. ft) of workspace, and to create between 85,000 and 182,000 new jobs. A 'Waterside City' is proposed at Deptford. Among the proposals that may now proceed is the 6000-unit new housing development at Barking Reach envisaged by Barking and Dagenham Borough Council, in association with the National Rivers Authority and private developers (Fig. 107). However, no new investment money was included in the announcement by the government and many observers have dismissed the proposals as wishful thinking. Typical of the comments was one from David Hall, the director of the Town and Country Planning Association: 'The Government is relying on the market to regenerate the area but that will never happen in a co-ordinated way'.[42]

108 *Ecological park at Cramley Street, which is preserved in the local neighbourhood's alternative King's Cross*

King's Cross

Since 1987, a debate has raged over proposals by British Rail and a number of landowners for a massive £3 billion office-tower-led redevelopment of the under-used site to the north of King's Cross and St Pancras stations in the north of London. Following the announcement by British Rail that the rail services from the Channel Tunnel would be extended to King's Cross, the developers, the London Consortium, appointed Foster Associates to prepare the master-plan. Strong local opposition to the proposals, particularly the concentration of office development, quickly led to formation of the King's Cross Railway Lands Group. These prepared alternative plans which were much more low-key, one of the important features being the preservation of the recently completed ecological park at Cramley Street (Fig. 108). The outcome of the differences of view has still to be determined but the developer's scheme is awaiting better times for investment.

4 The European experience

Introduction

While there is much to be learnt from the many years of American and British experience of urban regeneration, the European experience contains important lessons. The issues arising from de-industrialization are common across the whole of the western world as new technologies replace the old manufacturing and engineering industries; the ports of Hamburg, Rotterdam, Amsterdam, Genoa and Barcelona have the similar redundant docks to those in London, Liverpool, Boston and New York. The difference lies in the approach to finding solutions. In Britain and the USA, market forces, tempered by public pressure, have determined much of the present approach. In contrast, most European cities have a preference for strategic planning and greater public investment: 'Wherever you look in Europe, a new generation of cities is emerging, competitive and confident'.[1] Politicians and planners perceive their cities as single entities. National and City governments have made public funding available to stimulate investment for the refurbishment of the existing built environment and for the provision of new infrastructure at all levels – roads, railways, public transport, public buildings and spaces, housing and environment.

This chapter tries to show some of the best examples of urban regeneration practice in western Europe (Fig. 109). In so doing, it should reflect Catherine Slessor's poignant observation in *The Architectural Review* that 'The nature of the city is still an important European preoccupation'.[2]

109 *Classic waterfront development at the Oudehaven, Rotterdam.*

European funding for urban regeneration

The majority of public funding for urban regeneration in Europe comes from national and city governments. The European Union (EU) assists by making approximately one-third of its budget available to areas of greatest deprivation. The principal means of funding are the European Regional Development Fund (ERDF), which was set up to reduce regional imbalance in the community, and the European Social Fund (ESF), which has the task of promoting job opportunities for workers.[3] The criteria for the aid is that the average income per head of population in the Region is below 75 per cent of the Community average. In 1993 the EU planned that £113 billion would be available for a six-year programme. This will be distributed to the poorest Regions which are located in Spain, Portugal, Ireland and Greece. Northern Ireland and Merseyside will be the main beneficiaries in Britain. Germany has ensured that funds are directed towards east Germany, where the people's standard of living is only about 35 per cent of the average for the European Community.

The physical pattern of urban regeneration projects in Europe is similar to that of the USA and Britain. There is no significance to the order of countries and cities in this chapter. All those included have tackled their problems in their own way, but together they make up the current European urban regeneration scene.

THE NETHERLANDS

Neighbourhood renewal and housing

Urban regeneration has been a major political priority in the Netherlands, but it is in the renewal of the residential fabric of their large cities that the Dutch have most to show to the rest of the world. Many 'urban renewal districts' are characterized by acute social problems. In some districts up to 75 per cent of the working people are unemployed or on minimum benefit. Many have large ethnic populations which settled from Turkey, Morocco and Surinam. This inflow has greatly affected existing social structures. Social programmes have therefore been devised to improve the quality of life during and after urban renewal. The Town and Village Renewal Act of 1985 gave municipalities their own urban renewal funds. This finances property purchases, dwelling improvements, new facilities and infrastructure. It allows for the construction of new social housing and for the improvement of older housing. The work is managed through district project offices and project groups involving officials, residents and businesses for urban renewal areas. These prepare plans and submit them to the local authorities for approval and give a detailed report once a year. Dwellings are renovated where possible, but if demolition is the only answer, plans for new development are prepared. The rents for any new dwellings must be affordable within the limits of the existing residents, who are given first priority. In addition, new shopping and business accommodation and facilities are created wherever possible.

An allowance per dwelling is allocated by central government to cover the employment of a co-ordinator to work in the community. If no neighbourhood groups exist, the local authority encourages their establishment. Construction is expected to commence within a year to maintain the enthusiasm of the residents. Although in some instances it has proved difficult, the housing authority, whether this is the local authority or a housing association, designates the tenants (both from the neighbourhood and from outside) for the

110 *Rotterdam's Ten Year Plan of 1985. Reproduced by courtesy of Rotterdam City Council.*

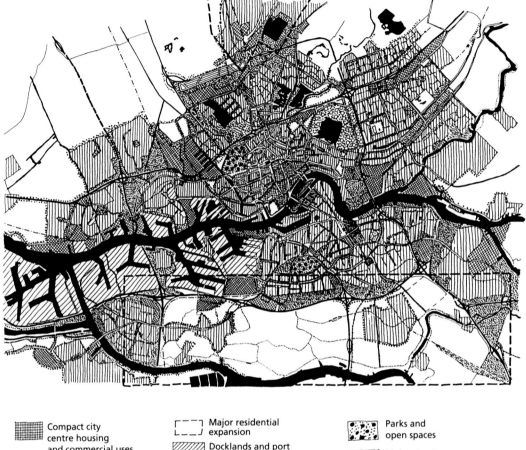

▓	Compact city centre housing and commercial uses	⌐⌐⌐	Major residential expansion	∴∴	Parks and open spaces
▓	Outer residential areas	⧄	Docklands and port uses	░	Major structure planting
		▦	New business development		

projects before the design work begins. This enables them to participate fully in the design process.

Rotterdam

Rotterdam is a most significant gateway into mainland Europe. The problems that have confronted the city in the past few years have been as acute as anywhere else in Europe or in America. The population is approximately 600,000 with a further 400,000 people living in the surrounding suburbs. Between 1960 and the early 1970s, Rotterdam lost 170,000 people to the satellite towns and attracted back only 15,000, many of whom came from the

Netherlands' former colonies. The city's fortune was traditionally based on its docks, both for ship building and trans-shipping. By the late 1970s this economy was rapidly in decline. The city had to take steps to broaden its economic base and to deal with the redundant land no longer required for heavy industrial use. Its plans are impressive (Fig. 110).

Urban regeneration strategy
The policy for urban regeneration in the city is radical and highly futuristic. Rotterdam is a city in which the people have been forced by past circumstance to accept change. The destruction of the city centre in 1941 created a state of mind

which has remained in existence to this present day. In its own publication, *Gateway Rotterdam*, the City Council writes: 'The examples, especially during the period after the Second World War, are well known to every Rotterdamer: the reconstruction with accent on work, city renovation with the emphasis on the function of living, and now Rotterdam is preparing to finish the job'.[4]

The strategy has two main directions: the first is aimed at creating opportunities for attracting new business and commercial investment into the city centre and on to adjacent redundant sites: the second associated with meeting social need, particularly in the area of housing and related uses. In 1985 the City Council produced a ten-year plan, the 'Binnenstadsplan' (Fig. 111), and subsequently the white paper 'Vernieuwing van Rotterdam' in 1987. These plans gave a framework to a policy for urban regeneration. Its principles are as follows:

111 *Housing in Rotterdam – urban renewal rings.*

Ist ring: prewar housing in the inner city

2nd ring: urban renewal a priority

3rd ring: early-post 1945 housing, some being improved

4th ring: garden city housing

112 *The Rotterdam Waterstad.*

tropical swimming pool, an Imax theatre (designed to project a super-screen film of Rotterdam and its port, together with exhibition space), old ships, walking routes, bars and restaurants have transformed the area. The climax of the redevelopment is at the Oudehaven, where Piet Blom's cube-shaped housing and the oldest 'skyscraper' in Europe, the White House – form the backcloth to a harbour filled with old barges (Fig. 112).

3 Leisure and culture: to refurbish and repair the streets and parks in the 'Park Triangle'. The plans include the construction of an Arts Centre and a building for the National Institute for Architecture. The funding for the new cultural buildings is from the government, whilst the land is being made available by the City Council.

4 Conference facilities: to develop these in the old harbour areas to the south of the city.

5 Kop van Zuid: to develop the Kop van Zuid (Head of the South) project on the south bank of the River Meuse. The new buildings in the development will include 5500 high-rise flats and other housing divided equally between rent and sale. The high-rise form of the development has caused the project to be called the 'Manhattan of the Meuse' (Fig. 113). It will also provide 60,000 sq. m. (646,000 sq. ft) of office space and 60,000 sq. m. of retail space, a major convention centre, a courthouse and hotels. The development will span the river with a new elegant suspension bridge into the centre of the city. The plan included for the refurbishment of the nineteenth-century Holland-America Line buildings and the huge warehouse De Vijf Wereddelen (The Five Continents). The finance for the development is from both public and private sources, with the majority of infrastructure funding coming

1 Commercial: to concentrate office development in the 'city triangle'. This area includes the Lijnbaan shopping centre, which is to be refurbished. Boulevards of over 25,000 sq. m. (270,000 sq. ft) office development and apartment buildings, hotels and conference facilities are being developed on a 'Manhattan' style.[5] The funding for the infrastructure is to come from government sources and the cost of the commercial development from investment by pension funds and insurance and from shipping companies.

2 Waterfront development: to develop a tourist maritime theme from the old harbours and waterways of the 'Water City'. The objective of the Rotterdam-Waterstad project was to provide new uses for the harbourside – following the movement westwards of the former dockland uses – and to link the river and the city. New housing, museums, a

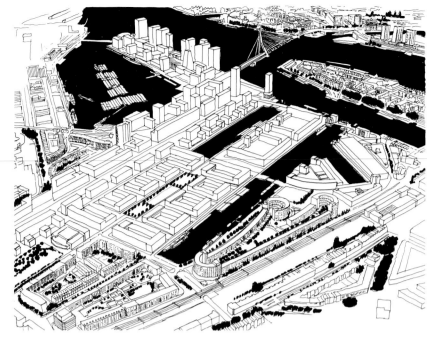

from central government, which will cover 85 per cent of the cost of the bridge and 50 per cent of the roads. The intention of the project is that it will of itself create employment and, in addition, open up the left bank of the River Meuse for further building and investment. It will also attract new companies to the city and provide an economic boost to the surrounding residential areas.

6 Transport: the construction of a three-kilometre tunnel in the centre of the city, to place the railway underground and to replace the 100-year-old bridges. This is estimated to cost 700 million gilders: the project will be completed in 1996 and will have taken nine years to implement.

7 Land ownership: Rotterdam City Council owns 60 per cent of the site. Ten days after the bombing in 1940, huge tracts of land were acquired for the purposes of eventual renewal. This makes the public/private partnership much easier to operate than in most British or American cities because the land can be made available as required. Moreover, the Netherlands government does not exercise detailed control over the expenditure by Rotterdam City Council.

8 Inner-city housing: from the early 1970s, an answer to Rotterdam's problems, as seen by the City Council, is to attract back the professional middle-class residents who had been encouraged to leave the city centre in the 1960s. This is to be mixed with new and refurbished housing aimed at attracting the young and the over-50s age group who are wanting to come back into the inner city. This will be in the form of mixed-tenure housing, where the balance between rented and sale housing will depend upon location.

At the heart of Rotterdam's plans is the philosophy of the 'compact city' and 'densification': a high density of buildings in a structured urban environment.[6] To

achieve this are policies to ensure that land is used efficiently. New housing is located where facilities such as schools and shops already exist. The construction of new housing on the waterfront has been possible in this context because the waterfront borders onto a number of old districts where all the support facilities are already present.

There are two additional aspects of Rotterdam's strategy that are important to the process of urban regeneration. First, the importance of the water frontage in townscape terms is enhanced by the presence of working inland waterways barges. Most of these are family-owned and have customary moorings when in Rotterdam. This imparts a dynamism to the environment that is missing from many dockland and riverside areas where efforts at regeneration are taking place. Secondly, the architectural style being used is not a replication of the vernacular and warehouse images that are so common in many other similar situations. The 'tree housing' and the 'pencil house', and the recently-constructed housing for homeless young people in the centre of the city designed by Mecanoo Architects, are all examples of an architectural language that is looking to the future (Fig. 114). These buildings aim to create the air of confidence in the future that is necessary to attract inward investment (Fig. 115).

Urban renewal in the old residential neighbourhoods

A most sophisticated programme of urban

113 *The Kop van Zuid – the Manhattan of the Meuse. Drawing by courtesy of Rotterdam City Council.*

114 *Young people's housing, Rotterdam. Architects: Mecanoo Architects.*

renewal has developed in Rotterdam: there are currently 22 separate designated renewal areas. Since 1974, when the renovation programme was introduced, a total of 45,000 pre-1914 housing units in the inner city have been purchased and either renovated or replaced. Some 50,000 dwellings have still to be tackled. These are programmed for completion by the year 2000. The areas that have benefited most from this action are Crooswijk, Cool, the Oude Westen and the Oude Noorden (Fig. 116).

The organization of the renewal process: half of the members of each project team are officials and half are local people appointed by the neighbourhood groups. The officials come from the Departments of Town Development, Housing, Building and Housing Inspection, Traffic and Transport and Social Affairs. The proposals are developed within financial guidelines laid down by the City Council. The architects are appointed by the project team usually after intensive interview sessions at which previous work is shown and working methods described. Project groups then write the briefs and act as clients throughout the building process.[7]

Standards of improvement: the standard of the renovation works varies widely. Large-scale studies are carried out in each neighbourhood to determine the kind of treatment required. There are three basic types of renovation: refurbishment,

supplementary renovation and major renovation.

1 Refurbishment is carried out on housing which will not be fully renovated within a period of three to seven years. The works include remedying defects, and in some cases installing a shower.

2 Supplementary renovation is essentially refurbishment supplemented by thermal insulation. Overdue maintenance work is done, the kitchen is re-equipped, and if necessary a shower is installed. The outer and party walls are insulated in order to reduce the energy costs of the dwelling. Supplementary renovation generally leads to a slightly higher rent for the tenants.

3 Major renovation, as the term implies, involves the radical renewal of the internal walls and partitions, often creating two new flats or apartments from three former ones. The attic level is converted into bedrooms, and central heating and insulation against both cold and noise transmission between dwellings is installed. The work is only undertaken with housing which can be brought up to a standard for less than 80 per cent of the cost of a new dwelling. Due to the reduction in the number of dwellings, it is therefore not always possible to rehouse everyone in their original locality, so new housing is constructed in adjacent areas wherever possible (Fig. 117).

If it is found that the foundations are prohibitively expensive to repair, the building is demolished immediately or, if it is not in a dangerous condition, it is scheduled for demolition within ten years. In this event, the dwelling is simply refurbished.

The tenants, who find it necessary to move out while the building work is in progress, are rehoused temporarily in other dwellings. If alternative accommodation is in short supply, they

can be housed in mobile homes which are moved from one neighbourhood to another as the need arises.

Social and environmental improvements: urban renewal is not, however, just a matter of renewing the housing stock. In addition, a whole new range of facilities (welfare, schools, shops, urban parks, play areas, etc.) have been constructed. It also involves a reshaping of the residential environment, local businesses and industries, and social and cultural amenities. Industries which create a nuisance are encouraged to move to other areas. Medium and small businesses are provided with new premises or financial assistance to enable them to survive. Most of the streets are upgraded to sheltered residential precincts (often converted into Woonerven: i.e. shared pedestrian/ vehicular areas in which the overall environment is designed to encourage traffic to travel at a slow speed), which involves the introduction of severe speed

restrictions, often linked with a one-way traffic system. Rotterdam's traffic management policy gives priority to public transport and cycling, and where it is thought necessary, measures such as bus-only routes and cycle paths are introduced.

Rotterdam's strategies are diverse yet complementary, because the two major strands of its urban regeneration plan are being developed together through an effectively-managed planning system. In this way, Rotterdam has arguably come close to achieving the best of both worlds, i.e. taking full advantage of private finance whilst pump-priming with public investment. However, the city is almost unique in the concern for communities in its nineteenth-century residential districts. Such a strong social orientation is rare in the approach to urban regeneration. If Rotterdam is able to devise and implement a strategy to assist inner-urban communities, why is it not possible for others to do likewise? The answer lies in

115 *Waterfront pavilion and restaurant on the Rotterdam waterfront.*

116 *Neighbourhood renewal in the nineteenth-century Noordereiland district of Rotterdam.*

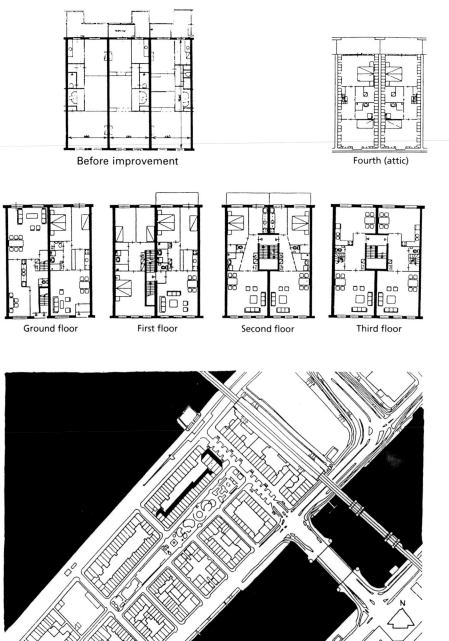

Before improvement

Fourth (attic)

Ground floor   First floor   Second floor   Third floor

117 *Houses and environment at Noordereiland. Architects: Leo de Jong Architecten.*

118 *Right: Amsterdam: figuregram showing tight pattern of urban streets and canals which the neighbourhood groups in the 1970s struggled to preserve.*

the belief of the politicians and the people alike in Rotterdam that the city must present a total image of itself. If their city is to compete against the major cities in other countries, and to prosper in the future, all of the projects are essential parts of the urban regeneration process. They are also strongly supported in this objective by the Dutch government, which sees Rotterdam's economy to be of crucial importance to that of the Netherlands as a whole.

Amsterdam

Amsterdam's active support programmes for rehabilitation and sensitive infill development have resulted in one of the most conserved cities in the world. Over the last two decades, much of this has been associated almost exclusively with the provision of 'social housing' for lower-income groups. The major developments are in the Neumarkt area to the south of Central Station and in Grote Wittenburgstraat, to the east of Oosterdok (Fig. 118).

Development in the Neumarkt area has reflected the protests in the early 1960s by neighbourhood groups against the

1 Neumarkt
2 Entrepotdok
3 Grote Witenburg
4 Mothers' House
5 Central Station

119 *Warehousing at Entrepotdok, Amsterdam, which has recently been imaginatively converted into housing.*

rationalist schemes of planners and developers, who wanted to demolish large areas of the city for road schemes and commercial development. With other architects and local people, Aldo van Eyck was instrumental in preventing further demolition. Their radical and immensely influential plan retained the existing traditional street pattern and scale, with shops and pedestrian movement threading along desired lines through courts and corners. The Wittenburg Island development is the largest and most recent development that has taken place in Amsterdam. An urban masterplan was prepared by the architects Arne van Herk and others in the late 1970s, but the new housing is undistinguished. The most significant project is at the Entrepotdok, where the old warehouses built between 1708 and 1829 have been converted into social housing. Without affecting the historic character of the buildings, the upper three levels have been carefully opened out at four locations to let in the light and to provide entrance to the flats on this level and above (Fig. 119).

A pattern of urban renewal similar to Rotterdam's has taken place and the

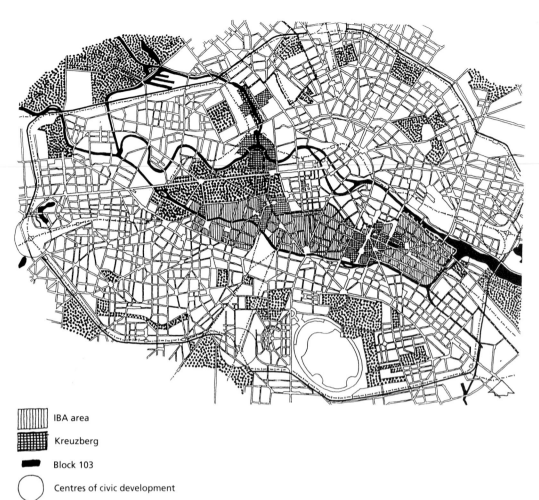

120 *Key development projects in Berlin.*

IBA area

Kreuzberg

Block 103

Centres of civic development

political strength of the neighbourhoods and the commitment of the City Council has been critical in its success.[8] In recent years, the policy has changed to accommodate the need for owner-occupation as well as the provision of sites for new international business and its housing needs.

GERMANY

Berlin

'Berlin is set to become the most dynamic European city of the coming decade'.[9] The reunification of East and West Berlin has released vast and desolate tracts of land for city centre development. There will clearly be a drive forward to use some of this land to make Berlin one of the world's leading financial centres and international architects are involved in a large number of projects (Fig. 120).

Renewal of residential districts

Most urban regeneration projects over the last ten years have been concerned with housing. Berlin has a long tradition in social housing. The development which established this reputation in the early 1930s – the Seimensstadt estate, which was built to a magnificent set of designs by Gropius and others – has been lovingly restored to its former glory. The overwhelming impression of the development today is that of peacefulness: 'Any skeptic from Britain or the United States, who believes that collective apartment schemes mean slum living . . . should see Siemensstadt and think again' (Fig. 121).[10]

From the mid-1970s urban renewal – primarily in four areas: Wedding, Kreuzberg, Charlottenburg and Schonenberg – became a major factor in Berlin's local government policies. Initially the methods were traditional, with no

121 *Walter Gropius's Siemensstadt housing in Berlin which still provides excellent housing.*

122 *New IBA housing in Berlin. Architects: Peter Cook and Christine Hawley.*

involvement of the local communities in the planning process. However, after much protest from house-owners who did not wish to sell their property or participate, legislation was introduced in 1972 to ensure that residents were fully consulted. The action swung away from wholesale demolition to the improvement of the existing housing and the environment, sensitive infill development and the incorporation of new schools, kindergartens and other social buildings to meet the needs of the community.

The Internationale Bausstellung (IBA)

The Internationale Bausstellung Berlin (IBA) of 1987 was organized to celebrate the 750th anniversary of Berlin. Its special brief – a 'caring approach to inner-city renewal' – was to relate a Building Exhibition to the real problems of inner-city regeneration. The aim was to 'rebuild the city of streets'.[11] The emphasis was to be on social housing, but high standards of design were not to be compromised. Designs frequently included the incorporation of low-energy measures and other green innovations. Heinrich and Inker Baller's project at Luisestadt and the infill development at Lutzoplatz, by British architects Peter Cook and Christine Hawley, are superb examples of the quality achieved throughout. However, some people in Berlin were highly cynical about IBA, considering it to be 'exaggerated' and 'useless' (Figs. 122 and 123).[12]

Kreuzberg

IBA was as much about the refurbishment of existing housing as new construction. Many of the new-build projects were constructed in relatively prosperous and leafy areas of the city. Much of Kreuzberg, in contrast, is intensely urban with the highest density in the former western part of the city. It is made up of imposing, but mainly crumbling, tenement blocks with a warren of passageways within. During the 1960s Kreuzberg was laid waste by grand motorway plans which were not finally abandoned until 1977. Thereafter, urban renewal in Kreuzberg became centred on the ability of the planners to preserve the 'Kreuzberger Mischung',[13] which could be translated roughly as the 'existing mixture of housing artisans, industry, trade and culture'. The population includes many different social classes, students and artists. It now accommodates a large Turkish population who have opened their own shops, restaurants and small-scale manufacturing businesses.

Kreuzberg also became the centre of issues concerning the illegal occupancy of empty tenement dwellings by squatters. In 1981, 20,000 flats were empty in Kreuzberg and awaiting what was a slow process of demolition. At the same time, 80,000 people in West Berlin were looking for housing. Riots occurred as the squatters protested at being ejected. The

result was a programme of immediate help from the City government to groups who wanted to modernize their dwellings.

The strategy for improvement includes the following elements:

1 The '800 DM Programme' to encourage the establishment of owner-occupier cooperatives amongst the people living in the tenements. The City Council subsidizes improvement works to the extent of 800 DM per square metre of existing floor space. Not less than 15 per cent of the cost of the improvement works have to come from the house-owners themselves, either through the carrying-out of building works themselves or by way of payment. Training is provided on-site so the people learn skills while refurbishing housing for their own ultimate occupation.

123 *Housing by Heinrich and Inker Baller which is generally considered to be the finest development of the IBA new building programme.*

124 *Block 103,*
Kreuzberg, Berlin.

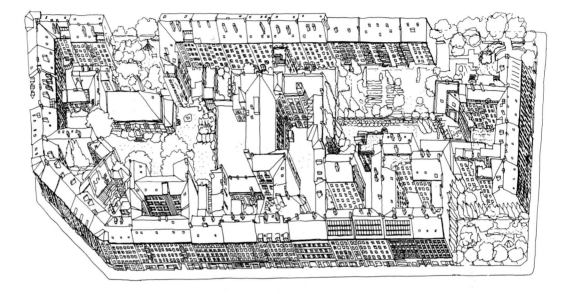

2   Self-help projects can be carried out by the residents themselves, with the aid of a grant of 70 per cent towards the cost of the materials where they carried out the work themselves and 35 per cent when they employed a builder.

3   The projects are aimed primarily at offering education and employment programmes to young people. This has developed into an important area of housing work in Berlin.

In 1979 the IBA Alt (old) was given the task for urban regeneration of two large parts of Kreuzberg, one around the Kottbusser Tor with 5000 flats and 10,000 inhabitants and the much larger area called SO 36 which includes 23,000 flats and 36,000 inhabitants. The policy determined was to conserve as much as possible, and enhance the area to make it tolerable to live and conduct business in. The task included the refurbishment of the buildings (or their demolition and replacement); the improvement of the environment; and the construction of new schools, kindergartens, an elderly people's home (at Kopenickerstrasse); a women's centre; a gymnasium; youth centres; a children's farm; new parks and

environmental traffic management. By March 1983, the West Berlin City government had agreed a twelve-point urban renewal programme. This included the requirement that the programme should be implemented with the full participation of the residents, be a gradual one, and respect the character of the area.

The process began by reusing empty buildings for temporarily decanting some of the residents. Others had short-term occupancy of some of the new housing constructed under the IBA programme. This way it was possible for 95 per cent of the people affected by rehabilitation to remain in the area; 61 per cent were accommodated back in their original flats.[14] IBA was able to modernize the houses at half the cost of new construction, which had the advantage of keeping the rents low.[15] Each city block of housing had its own architect appointed, who was responsible for the refurbishment programme.

The first priority was to make the properties structurally sound, as well as wind and watertight. Then kitchens and bathrooms were installed. The heating was geared to the ability of the residents to pay the cost of the fuel and this mainly meant the installation of a gas-fired system, to

125 *Grass walls protect the newly constructed park from the traffic noise. Note the solar collectors on the roofs of the nearby flats.*

126 *New balconies overlook greenspace in Kreuzberg, Berlin.*

127 *Right: The rear of Tommy-Weissbecker-Haus showing the murals which decorate the entire building.*

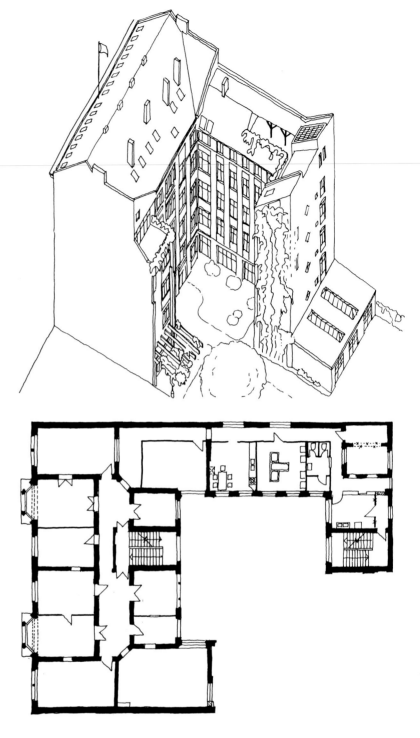

heat the living room and the kitchen. Very small flats were combined to make larger dwellings. Some parts of the tenement blocks in the courts within the city blocks were demolished to improve daylight levels to other dwellings.

Some of the smaller gap sites have been turned into neighbourhood gardens, including those on the corners of the blocks, where the housing had been demolished by Russian tanks in 1945. The pavements of some of the relatively broad streets have been widened, repaved and planted with trees.

In addition to these improvements,, much attention has been given to green issues. The whole of Block 103 (Figs. 124 and 126), which fronts on to Manteuffelstrasse and accommodates over a thousand residents, has become a testing ground for a series of unique pilot projects in energy generation, water and refuse recycling, greening the city, and the use of environmentally sensitive building materials (Fig. 125). It is envisaged that the £10 million project will devise practical solutions with low-running costs, suitable for widespread application in Berlin and the rest of Germany. Many of the projects have been carried out by companies set up by the squatters themselves, with skills acquired through their own self-help experience of re-building and renovating the buildings in which they live. Research and development has been funded by grants from both the Berlin and the Federal Government. Running costs are paid by the users.[16]

Another project at Willheima Strasse, in Kreuzberg, the Tommy-Weissbecker-Haus – which has been brightly painted on the outside – provides accommodation for young homeless people for up to a maximum of five years. The architects, Abram Mott and Harald Schöning, have converted the five-storey tenement house into 40 individual rooms with a cafe on the ground floor and a sports hall in the attic (Figs. 127 and 128).

East Berlin

Squatters have now settled into the crumbling tenement blocks of a number of residential areas in former East Berlin. Despite some significant efforts at refurbishment by the former city government, there are huge areas of housing that have received no repairs since the end of the Second World War. Bullet holes can still be seen, but – far worse than this – the symbols of Nazi revival can be seen on some of the buildings. For the new Berlin and German governments the task is to improve the living conditions, particularly of the young unemployed,

128 Tommy-Weissbecker-Haus, Berlin. Upper floor plans show the conversion into housing for young people. Architects: Abram Mott and Harald Schöning.

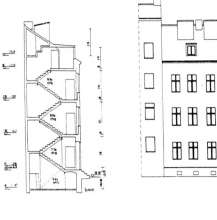

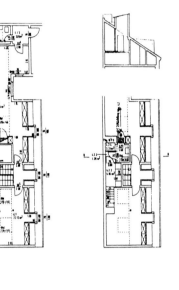

129 *Refurbishment of squatters' housing in the Lichtenburg of the former East Berlin. Architects: Marie-Jasee Seipelt and Paul Dlunzniewski.*

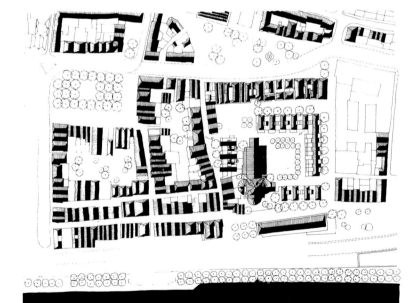

130 *The creation of streets and small squares around the Gross St Martin Church, Cologne; urban townscape at its very best.*

Cologne

Cologne is one of the oldest and most distinguished cities in Germany. The mixture of refurbished and new commercial and residential neighbourhoods in and around the city centre is an example of modern German architecture and urban planning at its best. From the east bank of the Rhine, the old city seems almost untouched. The river is fronted with beautifully restored buildings behind which flows an intricate complex of tightly-knit streets and squares which centre on the Gross Sankt Martin church. Yet amongst this is new housing built in the late 1970s which has rarely been surpassed in subsequent urban renewal projects in any country. The new housing retains the scale of the existing older buildings and its design respects tradition in a modern way without resorting to pastiche. Car parking is underground and the pedestrian spaces above, which are full of trees, fountains, and brick and stone paving, seem to grow out of and enrich the pattern of the old city. Restaurants, cafes and speciality shops all flourish (Figs. 130 and 131).[17]

The same quality of approach is evident in other inner areas of Cologne. South-west of the Severinsbrucke, the area around Dreikonigen Strasse and Zwirner Strasse is designated for urban regeneration. The new development, which is of very high quality, is mixed with refurbished nineteenth-century housing, small-scale businesses, and warehouses and industrial buildings that have been converted into housing. Dispersed throughout are new open spaces on cleared sites, including a new urban park (Fig. 132). The whole area is subject to a 30 km/hr speed limit. This is aided by a series of one-way streets, road narrowings, speed bumps, new planting, etc. Nearby, overlooking the Rheinau Hafen, a former granary warehouse has been imaginatively re-used to provide

before this kind of political movement takes hold. A number of housing organizations have set up projects to enable the squatters to improve the housing in which they live and, just as in Kreuzberg, they can earn a share of the ownership in return for their labour (Fig. 129).

131 *New housing around the Gross St Martin Church, Cologne.*

132 *Children enjoying a newly-created play space in Cologne. Note the refurbished housing behind.*

133 *The Speicherstadt warehouses in Hamburg, many of which have been converted into museums and housing.*

134 *Above right: A former granary warehouse in Cologne is being improved by its squatter residents with the aid of local authority funding.*

135 *The former Fishmarket building on the Elbe waterfront has been converted into a lively public space.*

housing for young people (Fig. 134). Initially taken over by squatters, the building has now been converted by them into permanent housing, music studios and rehearsal rooms, and artists' workshops. The City Council has given an 85 per cent grant for the building works and the remainder of the cost has been met by the young people's own labour.

Hamburg

The River Elbe is at the centre of Hamburg's urban regeneration proposals. As with all ports in Europe and the USA, the size and technical services of port installations have radically changed. However, unlike most other cityports, the shipping function has not moved from its original site and there is still a spatial relationship between the city and shipping. Unfortunately, the urban and port planning are rigorously separate from each other, which prevents the preparation of coherent policies for future development. However, the substantial neo-gothic style warehouses, built at the end of the nineteenth century along the waterfronts in the vast port district – the Speicherstadt – have recently been ceded by the Hamburg Port Authority to the City Council, which now has the responsibility to find new uses for the buildings. Some have been converted into museums and others into housing; but most significantly the complex of buildings with the canal system running in between the buildings remains intact, creating a unique image for the city (Fig. 133).

Significant improvements have been made to the extensive Elbe waterfront. The St Pauli Fischmarkt now stands on a refurbished waterfront which contains a mixture of new and refurbished former dockside buildings (Fig. 135). Most significantly, a series of new buildings appear as landmarks or a 'string of pearls'[18] on the north bank. The showcase is office development by architects Gruner

and Jahr, which was designed to accommodate a workforce of 2000 people (Fig. 136). A second building in a similar 'new engine-room aesthetic'[19] is the ferry terminal designed by William Alsop Architects of London and Me di um Architecten of Hamburg (Fig. 137).

Will Alsop credits his appointment as architect for the building to the 'Bauforums' or open architectural workshops staged by Hamburg City Council every year. These are spread over a four- to five-day period, during which a collection of 15 to 20 teams of invited architects develop a range of planning and urban design proposals to tackle the problems of different areas of the city in the vicinity of the port. The teams are composed of German and foreign architects from different schools of architectural thought, as well as younger local architects and students from German universities.

The new projects contribute considerably to the new image of the city.

137 *Will Alsop's ferry terminal overlooks the harbour.*

136 *Left: The Gruner and Jahr office building; one of the 'string of pearls' on the Elbe waterfront that are the focus of the city's urban regeneration initiatives.*

However, problems of great magnitude still remain, the largest being housing. The city's artisans and squatters are continually under threat from developers, 'and there is growing anger about the city's indifference to social policies in favour of commercial development'. This is despite the recent increase in social housing provision from 400 to 5000 per year.[20]

ITALY

Bologna

Bologna has been in the forefront of urban planning since the 1960s (Fig. 138). A significant factor in the city's approach was the ascendance of a government of the left, which has functioned through

neighbourhood councils. The primary objectives of their 'urban reformist' plan developed in the 1960s were as follows:

1   Growth: to resist the obsession with growth – of population, housing and industry – for its own sake.

2   Social and economic objectives: to seek a kind of urban planning which rejects the marginalization of working-class areas and creates a social mix within the urban fabric; also to focus on the quality of urban growth, with special attention paid to avoid overcrowding while at the same time designating large areas for green space. The economic significance of this policy is summed up by Professor Giuseppe Campos Venuti of Bologna University: 'The Bologna plan . . . sets out

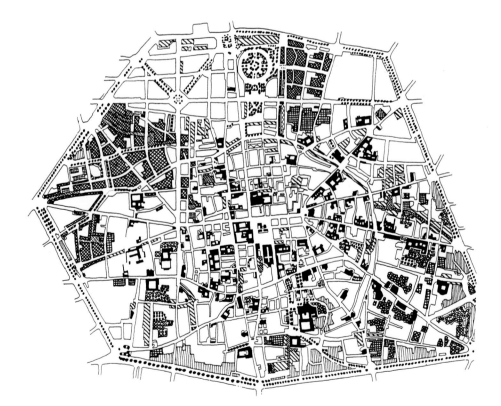

138 *The 1960 Bologna City Development Plan, which formed the basis for positive action: reproduced by courtesy of Bologna City Council.*

▨ Historic buildings
▨ Intensive new building or renovation
▨ Less intense development
▨ Land zoned for public use

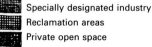

▨ Specially designated industry
▨ Reclamation areas
■ Private open space

140 *Principles of the restoration of the old neighbourhoods of Bologna.*

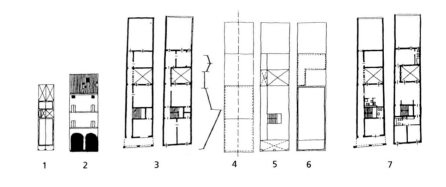

1 2 3 4 5 6 7

1 Concept

2 Elevation

3 Ground floor, typical upper floor and roof plan of dwelling before renovation

4 Model use of the ground

5 Typological elements (portico, porch, stairs, garden)

6 Identification of organic growth

7 Plans after renovation

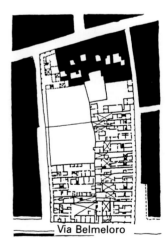

Via Belmeloro

139 *Left: Via San Leonardo, Bologna.*

to envisage a future urban system based on the belief that the quality of life is in itself a significant economic factor' (Fig. 139).[21]

3 Building restoration: Bologna City Council has made substantial funds available to restore buildings in the most run-down streets, which has stimulated private concerns to follow suit. Most revolutionary of all was the concept that conservation should encompass social as well as physical structure. In stabilizing houses, the programme was also stabilizing patterns of tenancy. The city expropriated the rundown buildings, renovated them, and then returned them to tenants' cooperatives. Under no circumstances were the tenants to be moved out and the dwellings sold to incoming people. This way, the council positively retained a vibrant community in the centre of the city. This unique experiment has had a lasting effect because it was tied to long-term instruments which survived the Communist administration. For most of the emulators there were too many variables to keep such programmes going beyond the next election.'[22] The approach to the restoration of the buildings was to use a morphological[23] and topological[24] analysis to provide both proposed demolition and reconstruction. In the areas of reconstruction, the general aim was to restore the fabric of the existing building to its former historic form by comparison with similar contemporary leading types. It is most significant to draw attention to the technique of assessing the work to be undertaken in the buildings to be refurbished. A considerable amount of the preparatory work was undertaken by young architects. The detailed studies of the buildings required large teams of trained workers: great use was made of the relatively large numbers of architecture graduates (around 60,000 yearly in Italy compared with 7000–8000 in Britain) all eager to gain practical experience (Fig. 140).[25]

A typical example of the project is the city block at Via San Leonardo, where previous building additions have been removed, the existing buildings have been renovated, and vacant sites have been infilled with new matching development. The central space was cleared of unwanted buildings and material, landscaped, and new walls built to separate the properties. The renovation programme has also been extended beyond the historic core of the city.

4 Employment: to stimulate ecological development and existing manufacturing industry, in response to industrial decline – rather than encouraging the speculative redevelopment of derelict industrial areas as practised by most cities in the western world. Bologna has a tradition of specialized industries which are adapted to the great artisan traditions dating back to the medieval period. This tradition is being maintained through the concept of 'transition shops'. These aim at keeping alive a number of professions and trades which are both highly specialized and culturally valuable, and which, if combined, could attract private and public use. These include, for example, the cabinet maker whose work is linked to that of the restorer, gilder, carpenter, inlayer, furniture polisher and chair mender; also the goldsmith, whose work is similarly linked to that of the engraver, silversmith and jewel setter. They are called transition shops because they help young people in the transition period between school and employment to create their own activity, a concept which is already practised in France and Germany. This is part of a positive policy of the City Council to maintain an extremely wide and flexible industrial base, through preventing the disappearance of the many traditional occupations and artistic activities whilst creating firms orientated towards new markets and the rapid invention of more sophisticated processes and products.

1 The Bigo
2 Covered performance area
3 Cotton warehouse
4 Aquarium

141 *Genoa Harbour and the development constructed to coincide with the 500th anniversary of the discovery of America by Christopher Columbus.*

142 *Above right: The 'Bigo', Genoa.*

5 Public transport: to encourage the use of public transport and walking in the city's 35 kilometres (21 miles) of arcades. In the 1970s, a comprehensive traffic management scheme was developed which is still in place. The concept is based on the principle of establishing highly differentiated street use. Less than a quarter of available street spaces are allotted to general use by traffic. Bus-only routes allow public transport into the more sensitive parts of the city centre. A major principle of the philosophy is that the provision of ever more parking facilities for ever more cars is out-dated, but it makes careful distinction between which types of journey should be facilitated and which types should be discouraged through design and regulation. Accordingly, along with severe limitations on long-term street parking, new parking facilities are provided on the outskirts adjacent to the major routes into the city,

with park-and-ride providing regular access into the centre. Park-and-ride schemes are well known in Britain and the United States but in Britain the deregulation of public transport works against the development of comprehensive policies on the Bologna pattern.

Genoa

Genoa is one of the major ports of the western Mediterranean, but by the 1970s the inner harbour had almost ceased to function as the shipping moved upstream. In the late 1980s the port authority, the City Council – supported by the national government – decided that the harbour should be transformed into an exhibition centre and become an attractive public amenity for the city. The work was to be completed in 1992, to coincide with the 500th anniversary of the discovery of America by Christopher Columbus, who was born in the city (Fig. 141).

The architect appointed was Genoa's own internationally-known Renzo Piano. His scheme combined new construction with the restoration of the existing historic buildings. The most dramatic of the new structures is the Bigo, which is intended 'to act as the symbol of the regenerated harbour'.[26] It is a most contemporary

structure, formed from tubular steel masts and cables supporting a tent roof above a performing area beneath (Fig. 142). Nearby, the new aquarium takes on the form of a ship, complete with funnels, galleries, bridges and cranes. The buildings which were renovated include the thirteenth- to sixteenth-century Palazzo di S. Giorgio with a typically Genoese painted facade, and a row of spectacular mid-seventeenth-century bonded warehouses. The long, former brick and rendered cotton warehouse – built in 1901 – was converted into a conference centre. The design of new workshops adjacent to the cotton warehouse is uncompromisingly modern, which contrasts with the sixteenth-century fortified gate nearby.

Renzo Piano's design demonstrates how it is possible to integrate the highest architectural ideals of the end of the twentieth century into the fabric of a historic city. His plans for the new metro stations in Genoa use a standard catalogue of parts with a clear discipline for a family of components. The first of these to be built at Brin consists of a raised steel frame with a curved steel and tinted-glass

cover over the platforms. The ticket offices are at the street entrance below. Completed in 1986, the station demonstrates the positive contribution that good design can make to new transport infrastructure and the improvement of the urban environment in general (Fig. 143).[27]

CZECH REPUBLIC

Prague

Prague is interesting to consider in terms of the role of conservation in urban regeneration. The city is one of the most beautiful in Europe. It has effectively remained unaltered for fifty years, but it is the first of the former communist block capitals that is finding it necessary to adapt

143 Above left: Renzo Piano's metro station at Brin, Genoa: a civilized building for civilized travel.

144 *Charles Bridge, Prague: The city is under threat from the changes confronting the former eastern part of Europe.*

could make it a business magnet for the whole of eastern Europe, with a potential catchment population of 400 million people. At present it is cheap to invest in the city and the city does not yet have the necessary environmental controls in place. Prague is not sufficiently wealthy for the City Council to turn away investment which creates employment opportunities and immediate income. Already foreign investment is resulting in the over-development of some sites.

There is in addition a huge problem of decay resulting from several decades of low investment. A total of 2700 of the city's finest buildings were taken over by the state in the years soon after 1948 and almost totally neglected. Large numbers of these buildings have been handed back to the owners or relatives of the former owners under the new government's policy of 'restitution', but the problem is that many of these people cannot afford to repair them. Prince Charles, in association with President Vaclav Havel, has established the Prague Heritage Fund to help to address the problem. Some progress in refurbishment is taking place but the scale of the problem is enormous.

quickly to change. Prague needs to develop into a western European-style city without destroying all the historic qualities that the tourists are flocking to see. The question is whether it can do both (Fig. 144).

Already developing are some of the less appealing visual aspects of consumerism. New enterprise and new money are displacing the old businesses and population. Everything is being geared to the tourists as grocery and butchers' shops become wine bars, bureaux de change, boutiques and antique shops. People are moving out as their housing is converted into hotels and restaurants, their local shops cease to exist and rents escalate.

Prague is tremendously attractive to western investors. Its architectural quality

EIRE

Dublin

Dublin possesses a fine group of Georgian buildings and a wealth of domestic interiors of great richness and variety. The symbol of this rich architectural heritage is undoubtedly the recently restored 200-year-old Custom House overlooking the River Liffey. Next door is the Financial Services Centre, one of the city's new flagship projects, designed by American architect Benjamin Thompson and Partners, to bring life back to derelict docklands (Fig. 145).

The overall scene is of crumbling buildings – the result of low investment

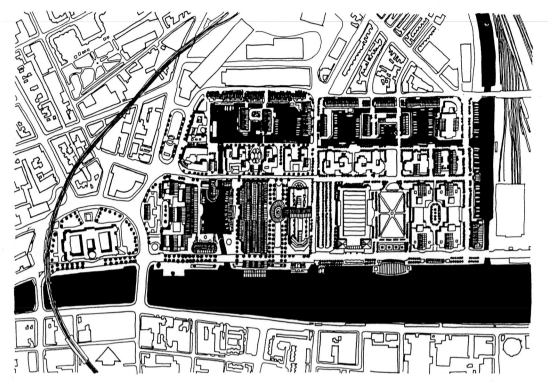

145 *Proposals by Benjamin Thompson Associates for the regeneration of the Customs House Docks, Dublin.*

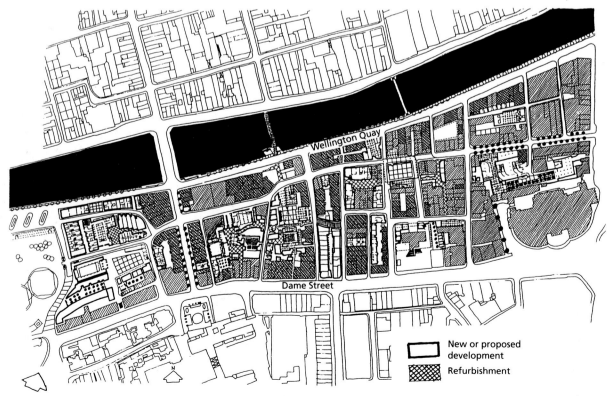

146 *The principles of the Temple Bar development.*

New or proposed development

Refurbishment

147 The Temple Bar, Dublin, showing improvements carried out to date. The sculpture was provided during the city's recent year as European City of Culture which brought much needed investment.

148 Above right: The new curved street. One of the many drawings in the Temple Bar report showing the integration of new modern designed buildings into the existing environment.

for many years. Outside the main retail and commercial areas it is impossible to ignore the dereliction of the Quays, the medieval area, and most of the inner city to the north.[28] The causes of this decline are familiar to many other European cities. Economically, the 1980s were one of the worst decades ever experienced in Eire. High levels of emigration and unemployment were evident. There were few investors who saw Dublin as a viable proposition – especially as there were no incentives, financial or environmental, to encourage action. Architecturally, however, this hiatus gave pause for thought. Instead of supporting large redevelopment schemes, Irish architects decided to restate the value of the traditional city of Dublin. The 1986 Urban Renewal Act created tax incentives to encourage development in the inner city, and the millennium celebrations of 1988 and the European City of Culture in 1991 firmly established civic pride. There now is considerable hope from recent developments.

Temple Bar: the most important

development is on the southern bank of the River Liffey. *The Architectural Review* wrote: 'Unlike the ambitious superstar master plans for Berlin and Genoa, the proposed rejuvenation of Dublin's Temple Bar area by a consortium of local architects is a much more low-key affair – yet its combination of responsive public space and mixed uses is an instructive paradigm for those involved in urban repair.'[29] The 12-hectare (30-acre) Temple Bar area (Fig. 146) contains a network of narrow streets extending from Trinity College and the eighteenth-century Parliament buildings in the east, to City Hall and Christ Church Cathedral in the west (Fig. 147). Until 1987 the area was subject to proposals for massive clearance and redevelopment. With the assistance of the European Regional Redevelopment Fund from 1991, a more gentle approach was encouraged. The brief for a design competition aimed at 'the design of public space – streets and squares, their sequence and proportions – acknowledging it as a subject crucial to the identity and physical character of the city'.[30] The competition also provided an opportunity to establish a collective planning framework that could enable and encourage individual users and private enterprise to participate in the renovation of the area.

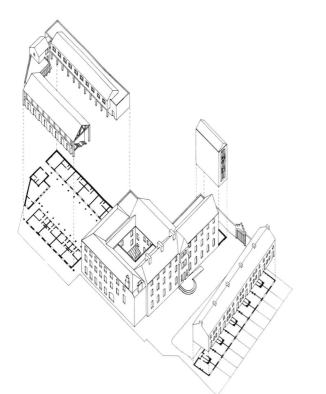

The winning design was by Group 91, a
consortium of eight Dublin architectural
practices.[31] The aim of their proposals was
not to produce a rigid masterplan to be
realized in a literal fashion but rather an
'integrated series of illustrative proposals – a
design guide – bound together within a
flexible framework, which will evolve during
the renewal of Temple Bar' (Fig. 148).

The strategies of the plan are as follows:

1   To accommodate a Temple Bar
community of 5000 citizens, including
3000 residents.

2   To reinforce a sense of place: not one
response, but a series of responses from a
mix of retained and proposed uses which
reinforce the existing street pattern.

3   Minimal demolition and imaginative
refurbishment, innovative responses to
opportunities for realizing the potential of
derelict sites.

4   A flexible framework for urban
development: based on a comprehensive
and realistic overview of the entire area.

5   Priority projects: flagship proposals for
each part of Temple Bar, including action

to strengthen the existing cultural
activities in the area and to construct a
Viking museum.

The project will benefit from a range of
tax-based incentives for the construction
and refurbishment of property which
includes a 100 per cent tax relief for
owner-occupiers on the cost of
improvements.

There are many other signs of positive
hope. Although not part of the proposals
for the Temple Bar area, the Irish Film
Centre, by architects Sheila O'Donell and
John Tuomey, is the first new building to
be completed in the area since the Group
91 framework was adopted and it has, to
some extent, acted as 'an indirect standard
bearer for Temple Bar's urban renaissance'
(Fig. 149).[32] The building has a strong
affinity with the approach advocated by
Group 91 – 'patient, invisible mending, as
opposed to brute cauterisation of the
existing urban fabric'.[33]

6   Homelessness: great efforts are also
being made to improve housing conditions
and to reduce the level of homelessness in
Dublin. Through a combination of the
refurbishment of buildings donated by the
Sisters of Charity, and a sensitively
designed courtyard extension, architect
Gerry Cahill has created a project for
Focus Point at Stanhope Green which
does much to raise the dignity of its
formerly homeless residents (Fig. 150).

FRANCE

The Parisian 'Grands Projets', which
commenced with the Centre Pompidou,
completed in 1977, have had a profound
influence on attitudes towards the city
throughout the world. Le Parc de la
Villette, Le Grand Arche at la Défense,
L'Institut du Monde Arabique, the new
Finance Ministry and the Pyramid at the
Louvre (Fig. 154), are but the most
prominent expressions of an explosion of

architectural activity which have helped to
focus the attention of the world on Paris.
For cities close by such as London, where
there are no similar plans for the city
centre, President Mitterand's intention to
make Paris the financial centre of the
world could present a serious threat: in
giving Paris an image of confidence in the
future he has taken an important step in
achieving this.

While the Grands Projets are important,
a number of more individually modest
projects by the Paris City Council and
other municipalities constitute the most
crucial element of French urban
regeneration during the last decade. These
initiatives are important to the future of
urban life for the romantic vision of
France, 'that sees it still in terms of an
idyllic countryside and solidly bourgeois
towns providing a foundation for a Paris
that personifies the superiority of French
culture'[34] does not portray what is really
happening. People are moving into
suburbia and the countryside in just the
same way that they are in Britain and the
USA. Hypermarkets and other mass
retailing outlets abound on the outskirts of
towns and cities. 'Shedlands is a
monumental disaster,' says F. A. Pater, in
his article in *The Architectural Review*.[35]
He also advises that the consequent lack of
demand in the historic town centres has
kept shop rents affordable, enabling types
of shop to survive which have ceased to
exist in Britain and the USA. However,
despite this the town centres 'superficially
stimulating, are actually dying fast –
outside the brief tourist season, restaurants
and cafes are frequently empty even at
weekends. The outward forms of urbanity
remain but the substance has
evaporated.'[36]

To address this decline, the cities are
making considerable efforts to regenerate
their inner urban areas. At Lille there are
redevelopment proposals for 120 hectares
(50 acres) of hotels, conference centres and
housing around the railway station,

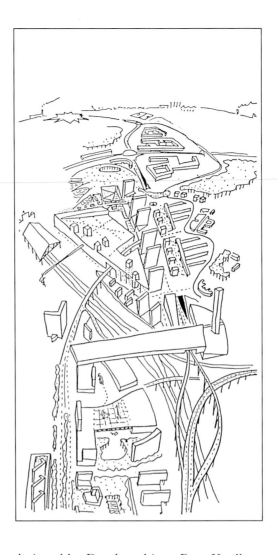

151 *Impression of urban regeneration proposals, Lille, France. Architect: Rem Koolhas.*

designed by Dutch architect Rem Koolhas
(Fig. 151). Lyon has its own Grands
Projets, including the restoration of Tony
Garnier's Grande Halle. The mammoth
new inner-city neighbourhood at
Montpellier by Ricardo Bofill and the
impressive new keynote buildings at
Nîmes by Norman Foster and Jean
Nouvel illustrate the determination of
most French cities to build for the future.

Paris

Urban renewal strategy

Industry in Paris was located in the east of
the city, downwind of the smart 'quartiers'.
Since people were much less mobile in the
nineteenth century, the working-class
districts were located near big industry.
Today, the heavy industry has gone but the
east end is being revitalized with new
projects such as the complex of new and
refurbished buildings in the Parc de la
Villette, the Opéra de la Bastille, Le Théâtre
National de la Colline, new sports stadia
and parks such as Le Parc de Bercy
overlooking the River Seine (Fig. 152).

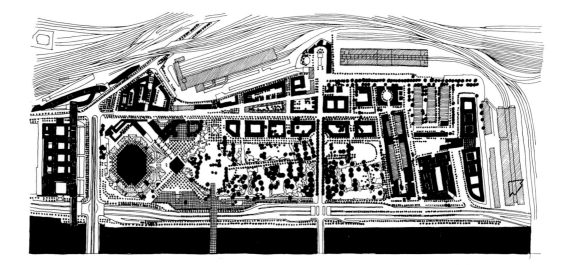

152 *Parc de Bercy, Paris.*

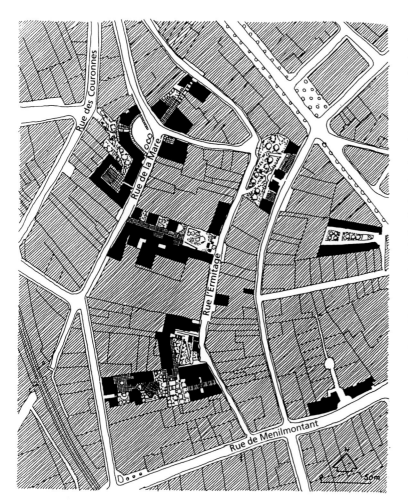

153 *Small scale interventions in the east of Paris.*

The process of transformation which has taken place in the east of the city and throughout Paris during the last decade was made possible by the presence of a large number of abandoned sites. Almost all of the new projects have been built on land occupied by former industrial buildings, railroad tracks and freight depots. The objective, announced at the end of the 1970s by the mayor of Paris, Jacques Chirac, was to improve the quality of the depressed areas. The programme endeavoured to encourage a mixture of housing, commerce and public services. All developments were to be designed to respect the existing streetscape.

There are two spectacular aspects to this mammoth-scale programme. First of all, Paris is building up its cultural image – but it was a bold decision to place the new buildings in the run-down parts of the inner city. The action has, however, succeeded in encouraging further investment from the private sector. Secondly, the plan is concerned not only with buildings but also with a revaluation of public spaces and areas. These are based on ideas of easily identifiable urban spaces: parks, streets, tree-lined boulevards and promenades, squares, parks, riverfronts, and the complexity of the Paris of Haussmann, with its city

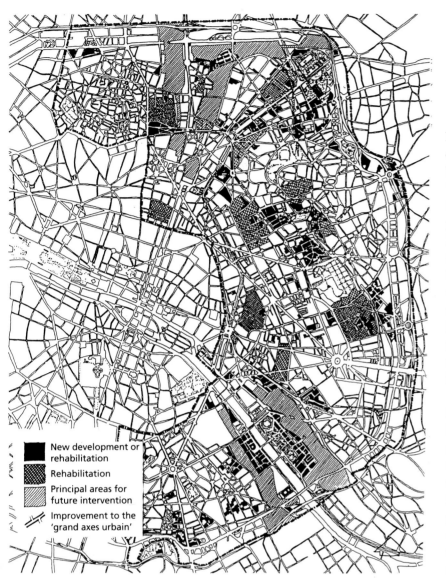

New development or rehabilitation

Rehabilitation

Principal areas for future intervention

Improvement to the 'grand axes urbain'

155 *Plan de l'Est, Paris.*

154 *The Pyramid at the Louvre.*

has two phases. The first, which includes consultation with the local residents, businesses and organizations in the 'Quartier', is managed by the City Council. The process includes the preparation of a Plan d'Aménagement de Zone (PAZ) which is made up of a graphic document, a volumetric plan defining the boundary of the proposed ZAC, and, within it, the distribution of future land use, public open space, roads and footways, together with the frontages and plot ratios to be achieved by new development within maximum specified height limits, and other guidelines.

After the approval of the PAZ by the Paris City Council the second phase begins: the architectural study and realization of the design. This is often organized through architectural competitions. After analysing the feasibility proposals, the City Council produces an 'urban design' (Fig. 153), a definitive project, and passes it on to the operative phase, entrusted to the Société d'Economie Mixte d'Aménagement de la Ville de Paris (SEMAVIP). This is a joint public/private sector company backed with public investment. It acquires the land and property for the developments.

Development can be by public bodies, cooperatives, and private companies, or a combination of these. The SEMAVIP is the organization through which the different sectors come together. The procedure works successfully because there is usually public sector funding available to support the principle that there should be public uses in redevelopment proposals; it is also successful because of the participation of the City's public sector agencies throughout the process which ensures that they have a real influence in determining the character of the urban project. It is important to recognize that the division between public and private spheres is not so sharply demarcated in France as it is in Britain and the USA. This enables public bodies and the private

blocks, internal courtyards and passages (Fig. 154). It is a plan which appreciates the value of urban design as essential to regeneration.

Plan Programme de l'Est

The plan for the east of Paris was put into operation in 1983 when the Paris City Council approved the 'Plan Programme de l'Est de Paris'. This is a planning tool affecting seven arrondissements which aims to create a better economic equilibrium between the east and the rest of the city (Fig. 155).

The major instrument used to implement the plan is the Zone d'Aménagement Concerte (ZAC). The ZAC is a procedure for urban regeneration in city neighbourhoods where there are substantial new build and/or refurbishment projects involving the use of public land and public building uses. It

sector to work freely together, regardless of political doctrine.

The plan has been successful but it has become clear that it cannot address the wider problems of Paris; projects such as La Villette are significant but they fail to tackle the major problems of social deprivation and long-term unemployment. Furthermore, the present government in France is now favouring a more low-key approach, with greater concentration on the protection of the past.

The architectural guidelines

The launching of the ZAC projects at the end of the 1970s coincided with the emergence of a new French architectural culture. There is now a generally accepted view that the form of new development should work into the established urban fabric as illustrated in (Figs. 156 and 157). The street, the city block, and the idea of the history of the physical fabric of the city were the notions upon which to build the 'Ville Sédimentaire': the city which grows upon itself in a permanent process of adaptation of the built urban heritage. The new regulatory plan re-established a linguistic continuity with the traditional Parisian regulations which existed from 1784 to 1902. Rules for street alignments reappear, as do limitations regarding the height of buildings and the division of land. The former parcelling of development was replaced by a process of edification open to the intervention of many promoters and architects, both public and private. This has caused some difficulties with design coordination. The process now envisages the appointment of a single architect, whose task is to prepare a series of detailed indications of the composition of the overall development, and then to coordinate the work of the other architects within this framework. The role of the city planner is not so much that of establishing a certain number of restrictions and norms, but rather to encourage a collective working process amongst the architects.

156 *Urban intervention at 100 Boulevard de Belleville, in the east of Paris.*

157 *Plan of the development at 100 Boulevard de Belleville, Paris, showing the careful integration of the new development into the existing built environment.*

1 Project within its
  city block
2 Ground floor
3 First floor

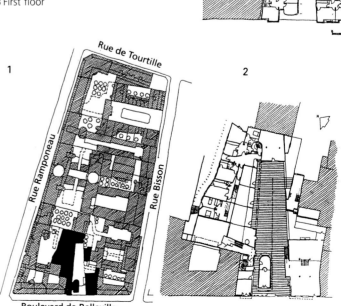

158 *Parc de la Villette, Paris.*

The construction of new housing in the ZACs is helped considerably by the common concensus in France that there is a need for public investment in housing development, whether this be for subsidized rent or for purchase with assisted mortgages. Furthermore, the financial institutions consider housing a worthwhile investment and both the public and private sectors have determined that Paris should not become the exclusive preserve of the rich. Both see the provision of housing for low- and middle-income groups as essential to the regeneration of the city.

Parc de la Villette

The new 35-hectare (68-acre) Le Parc de la Villette is the largest park in the city (Figs. 158 and 159). It is now one of the major cultural and tourist attractions. Located in the park is a sequence of new buildings including les Cités des Sciences et de l'Industrie, la Géode (an Imax Theatre) and la Grande Halle which was created in the former abattoir, a construction of iron and glass erected in 1867. This now accommodates trade fairs,

exhibitions and functions requiring a large space. Other buildings in the park are Zenith – a rock music hall – Le Théâtre Paris Villette, seating 300 people which has been constructed inside a former stock exchange building, and two new major buildings, le Conservatoire and la Cité de la Musique.

To the south of the Parc de la Villette, on the Place de la Bastille, is located the 2700-seat Opéra de la Bastille, designed by the Canadian architect Carlos Ott. This large and impressive building has provided a focal point for the economic revival of an area that was formerly a very run-down part of the city (Fig. 160).

The Bassin de la Villette and the St Martin Canal

The Bassin de la Villette was constructed in 1826 as part of a network of canals which were originally intended to feed the city's fountains with water. It measures 700 × 70 metres (230 ft × 23 ft) (Fig. 161) and served shipping, until the industrial decline in the 1950s led to the basin gradually becoming abandoned and its vast warehouses and sheds becoming redundant. Most of the former buildings have been

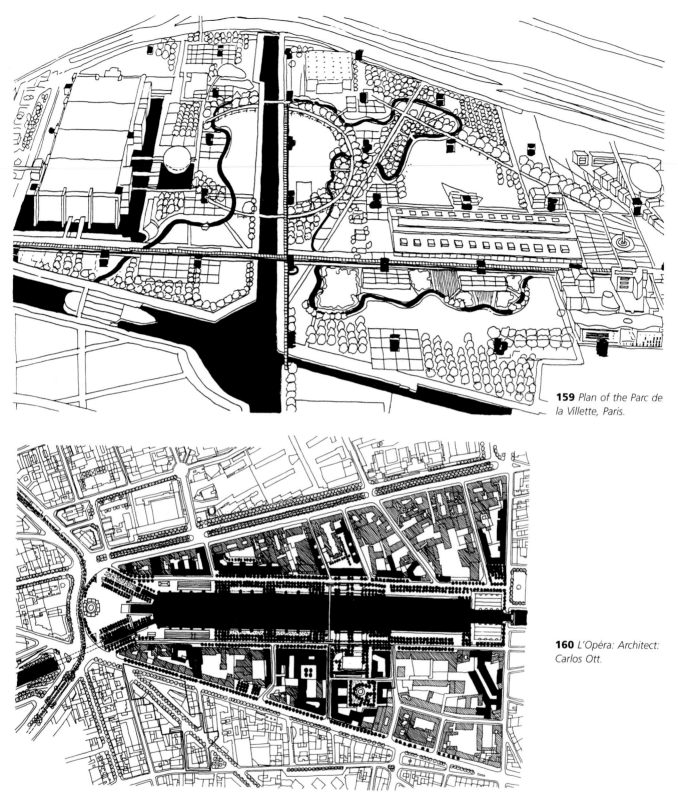

159 *Plan of the Parc de la Villette, Paris.*

160 *L'Opéra: Architect: Carlos Ott.*

demolished but some remain standing. The beautiful Rotonde de Ledoux has been restored and the area around at La Place de Stalingrad completely transformed into a splendid public place. The project is highly successful because a fine balance has been achieved between the industrial past and the Bassin's new role as a recreational area (Fig. 162). Industrial romanticism has not been allowed to dominate and the traces of the past have

not been erased.

The St Martin canal, which leads off the Bassin to the north, has also been renovated and its iron bridges and locks repaired. It now provides a most important element of infrastructure to this otherwise insignificant part of Paris.

161 *Plan of the Bassin de la Villette, Paris.*

162 *The Bassin de la Villette at which a fine public space has been created.*

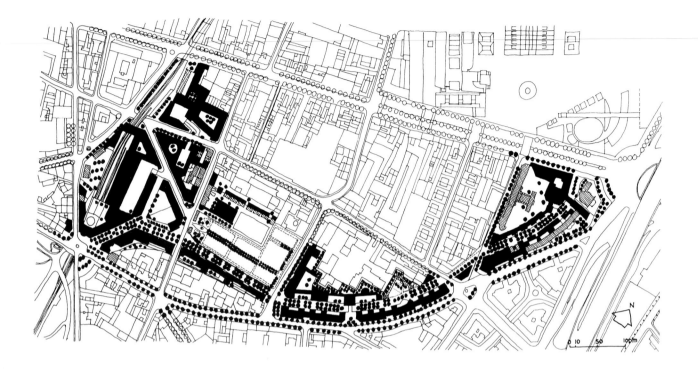

The Manin-Jaurès ZAC

In the same area of Paris, a disused railway line was purchased in 1982 by the City Council from the French State Railways (SNCF) and converted into a 20-metres wide and one-kilometre long city promenade, linking the new Parc de la Villette in the north with Hausmann's Buttes-Chaumont park in the south (Fig. 163). The mall very quickly became the catalyst for major urban renewal in the area. The treatment of the new pedestrian mall and of the façades of the new buildings fronting the mall were the subject of an architectural competition in 1986, which was won by Alain Sarfarti. He was then commissioned by the SEMAVIP to design the mall in detail for the City of Paris and to coordinate the designs of the eight teams of architects appointed for the buildings fronting the mall. For critical points such as corner houses or large areas of land, joint studies by these architects were put in hand so that several potential solutions could be compared.

The new housing includes both flats for rent and sale. Some of the housing has shops, and there are studio workshops on the ground floor. To the north, Alain Sarfarti's viewing platforms afford extensive views over the Villette cemetery. Here are located a new elementary school and a nursery school designed by Alain Sarfarti, and a public garden (Figs. 164 and 165).

The Parc Citroën

In the south-west of the inner area of Paris, the site of the former Citroën factory has been redeveloped to form a new heart for that part of the city. The axis of the Rue Balard defines its eastern boundary which is flanked on either side by new housing, offices and a hospital. The park is laid out in a formal manner (Fig. 167). In the centre is a large green leading down to the railway which separates the park from the River Seine (Fig. 166). To one side, a series of small gardens, each laid out in a different manner, contrast with the formality of the main space. A large part of the park has been designed as an ecological area with different species of plants and grasses (Fig. 168). The new housing and other

163 The overall plan of the converted railway in the Manin-Jaurès ZAC, Paris.

164 The Manin-Jaurès ZAC. After only a short period of time the new street has become very mature.

165 The new school fits into the urban street. Architect: Alain Sarfarti.

buildings are four and five storeys in
height, which provides an effective scale to
frame the open space. The architectural
design reflects the new thinking in Paris
and the overall effect is very distinctive.

Montpellier and Nîmes

Montpellier and Nîmes (populations
212,000 and 130,000 respectively) have
both embarked on a number of dramatic
urban renewal projects which are very
different in form. Both cities are anxious
to attract the new technology industries
wishing to locate in pleasant surroundings
on cheap land which they can offer. To
create the necessary impetus to attract new
businesses into their cities, the two
entrepreneurial mayors – Bousquet in
Nîmes and Frêche in Montpellier –
considered it of paramount importance to
enhance the image of their cities. The new
development, which they envisaged, had to
be of the highest quality so internationally
known architects were appointed –
Ricardo Bofill, Jean Nouvel and Sir
Norman Foster. 'Imagine the conservative
councillors of Bath planting a "Bathonian
Beaubourg" beside the Roman baths,
inviting an Italian to build a vast stadium
(to house a not very good football team),
and commissioning a council block that
looks like a ship and feels like a palace. Or
the burghers of Bristol connecting their
post-war concrete city centre to 1700
hectares of mixed-use development in
bizarre Classical clothing. Such has
happened to Montpellier and Nîmes.'[37]

Mayor Bousquet's initially modest plans
for urban renewal grew rapidly into
massive schemes for rehabilitation,
infrastructure planning and the
construction of monumental buildings that
mirrored President Mitterand's in Paris.

The new Library and Art Gallery, by
Norman Foster, is described in *The
Architectural Review* as a 'new civic temple
of culture' and a 'refined, modern abstract
of a Roman monument'.[38] The new

166 *The water jets in the Parc Citroën.*

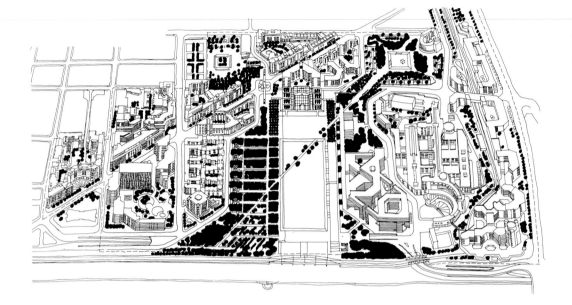

167 *The Parc Citroën, west Paris. The park is laid out in a formal manner.*

168 *Parc Citroën: overall view.*

169 *Norman Foster's Museum in Nîmes, France.*

170 *HLM, Nemaussus 1 and 2, designed by Jean Nouvel – Image architecture in Nîmes.*

building stands next to the Maison Carrée, one of the best preserved Roman temples in the world (Fig. 169).

Further projects include the renovated eighteenth-century Jardins de la Fontaine and other city spaces, the removable roof over the Roman Arènes, the new Stade des Costières, and the 'stupendous (initially shocking)' HLM housing, Nemaussus 1 and 2, designed by Jean Nouvel. The bright façades are reminiscent of steamships. Each of the two parallel blocks of housing have 114 apartments of one, two and three bedrooms. Three galleries made of perforated corrugated sheet metal run along the elongated structures of the two parallel blocks, and access to the apartments is from these galleries, or by lift.[39] Each apartment has a private balcony on the south side. There is a strong sense of community amongst the residents, who clearly enjoy living in such a unique development (Fig. 170).

Mayor Frêche of Montpellier has perhaps been even bolder. Ricardo Bofill's Antigone development (Fig. 171) can only be described as spectacular. It extends a kilometre eastwards from the city centre to beyond the river. It consists of six-storey housing for social rent and for sale. These dwellings have been designed on an axis around a series of square, curved and polygonal spaces (Fig. 172).

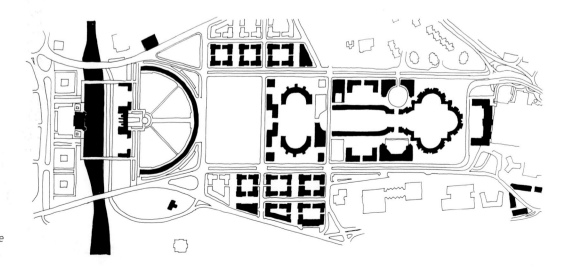

171 *Classical plan forms in the plan of the Antigone development.*

Antigone is, however, merely the largest of a string of projects that form part of a total revamp of Montpellier. Mayor Frêche's plans are to join the city with the sea two miles away with 1700 hectares (4200 acres) of expansion. This will include the construction of Port Maranne, to be designed by Bofill, which will be a mixed-use development centring on a newly created port and huge park. Frêche plans numerous sports and cultural buildings, including an Olympic swimming pool by Richard Meier and an opera and conference centre by Claude Vasconi. He proposes the creation of 'Lez vert' (natural parks) and to develop the city's important 'technopoles' (science parks); also to build on Montpellier's reputation for medical research.

SPAIN

Barcelona

Olympic Games buildings

The staging of the Olympic Games in 1992 changed Barcelona dramatically. The building plans were different from any that had been implemented by any other host city. Rather than locating them on a choice site in the suburbs, they were linked with the regeneration of run-down industrial land in the centre of the city. In this way, the accommodation built for the competitors in the Olympic Village was intended to be part of the city and have a lasting effect as housing for the people. The principle behind the location of the sports complexes was that they should be spread over a number of sites within the city, but linked to one another with a new outer road system. This enabled the games and the facilities to embrace the whole of the centre of the city.

The stadia were located on Montjuic Hill, where an Olympic stadium had already been built in 1929, with an eye on the 1936 games. The stadia are set in

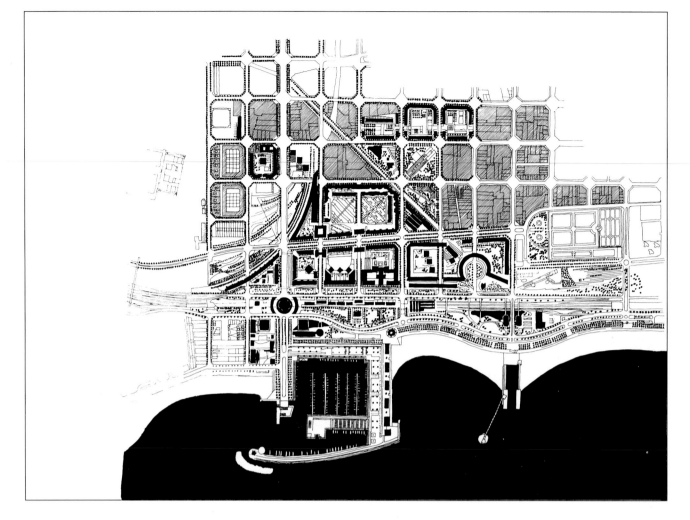

173 *The plan of the Olympic Village.*

174 *The design of the open spaces is one of the most significant achievements.*

175 *The new housing in Barcelona's Olympic Village is set in a highly civilized environment.*

a formal park and are crowned by Santiago Calitrava's telecommunications tower, which rivals Norman Foster's similar structure on a distant hill.

The Olympic Village

The central concept of the design of the residential Village was to plan it as a natural extension of the city's structure of roads and city blocks, conceived by Ildefons Cèrda in 1859. The Passeig de Charles I runs through the village from Gaudi's Sagrada Familia to the sea, where it is flanked by two 44-storey tower blocks. Between the new housing and the sea, the new Park de Mar has been laid out along the entire length of the waterfront. The result is perhaps the most remarkable piece of built urban city this century

(Figs. 173 and 175). The feature that makes the development so successful is the design of the public spaces (Fig. 174): the new harbour, the tree-lined boulevards, the parks, the incidental spaces in the residential areas, the street art and sculpture, the play spaces and small seating areas and so on. These all make up a highly civilized city environment. The provision of new open space has not been confined to the Olympic areas, as they feature throughout the city, particularly in areas of poor or declining environment.

There is an amazing variety of new housing, most of which surrounds the perimeter of each city block, leaving a large central space in the middle. The curve of a former railway which is now in a tunnel has been reflected in a most elegant 550-metre (1800-ft) curve of housing (Fig. 177). The greatest problem seems to have been the disposal of the dwellings after the games were over, as many were still unoccupied a year later. Some of the ground floors of housing blocks, presumably intended for shops and cafes, were also empty. Within the development, and particularly on the inner edge of the village, the integration of the new housing with the existing housing, schools, factories, etc., is sensitively handled; it is a lesson for city planners to follow.

There were other projects carried out at the same time within the inner-city areas of Barcelona which may be of more direct benefit to the communities in which they are located. The former Catex factory (Fig. 179), one of the oldest buildings in the Poble Nou residential district, demonstrates the potential of old buildings for new uses, in this instance a sports and cultural centre. Nearby, the former Olivetti works built in the 1950s has been converted into an enterprise creation centre and workshops (Fig. 176).[40] Close to the railway station, former industrial land has been converted into a fine urban park (Fig. 178).

It is estimated that between 1987 and 1992, the Olympic Games generated more than £4.5 billion of total spending, creating 130,000 jobs. The result is a city that has been transformed. Much of the expenditure went on projects that will have long-term economic benefits to the city. Barcelona is the most significant example of urban regeneration arising from a city hosting a major sporting event. It is to be hoped that others will benefit in the same way in the future.

176 *The former Olivetti works in Barcelona, which has been converted into an Enterprise Centre.*

177 *A large curve of housing follows the line of the former railway.*

178 *A new urban park has been created close to the railway station in the inner area of Barcelona.*

179 *The former Catex factory in Barcelona, which has been converted into a social centre for the local community.*

5 Reflections

The previous chapters have shown the different dimensions of urban regeneration, which has clearly become an important issue for most countries in the western world. The successes are praiseworthy but experience clearly shows that there is no simple, magic formula or quick fix solution. Most of the best examples described have come from a fostering of creativity in whatever form it happened to appear in a given city at a given time. The cities that have been most successful are those that have recognized the different potential opportunities and have harnessed the energies of the people concerned.

A factor that is abundantly clear is that there is a role in the implementation of urban regeneration for many different types of organizations, whether they be the 'top-down' Corporations established by central or local government or the 'bottom-up' local neighbourhood group. There is often advantage in the city authorities taking on the coordinating role but the 1960s showed that an over-commitment to a highly-structured approach to urban renewal failed to meet society's needs. On the other hand, the future wealth and welfare of the inner cities cannot be left to under-researched and uncoordinated efforts of the private sector.

A balance between public care and private enterprise is needed. A theme that emerges repeatedly is that ordinary people can be trusted to help themselves provided that they are given the encouragement together with the necessary tools. However, nothing can be achieved without enlightened leadership, which must start at the level of central government. What can be said of the people who have provided information for this book is that there is a great sense of determination to succeed. All recognize the uphill struggle that they face. Most plead for more time and support from their government.

There are a number of factors that can dramatically help the urban regeneration process. Most require political willpower to achieve. Firstly uneven economic growth between the inner city and the outer areas can be controlled by planning at metropolitan/regional level.

Secondly, urban regeneration cannot succeed without investment in inner-city housing. This includes the provision of well-designed housing for rent which is affordable by all the people who live in the inner city. In this respect there is an urgent need for governments to give help to meet the housing needs of low-income people and ethnic and minority groups. The new housing should be designed to densities appropriate to the situation and should include development at densities lower than previously existed. In places where there is sufficient land there may be a place for 'urban villages'. However, these need to be diverse and designed to provide a balanced community. A key ingredient must be a continuation of the neighbourhood improvement programmes that have been so important in most countries. The housing policies will need to reflect the demographic changes in society. An important factor will be the nature of the forthcoming generations of young people. Outward migration may well continue in more prosperous economies, but elsewhere the trend could

180 *Urban regeneration of the highest quality at Aker Brygge, Oslo.*

halt as young people find it more difficult to find employment and purchase their home in the suburbs and beyond. They will need good housing to rent in the cities. This has always been accepted in continental European countries but it is only slowly being recognized in Britain and the USA.

Thirdly, it is obvious that the new hi-tech industries which most cities strive to attract cannot offer employment to large numbers of people. Nor can the growth of small businesses fill the gap. What is required is a new concept for work which can offer a sense of purpose to the individual. Except in a few cases, most politicians shy away from this very real need. Fourthly, land ownership and land values need to be addressed in a realistic manner. Public ownership of the land or a simple system of land acquisition at a reasonable price can be a great advantage.

Fifthly, cities are important to the well-being of countries as a whole. For this reason, the regeneration of the inner cities should be an integral part of government policies for economic recovery – rather than waiting for better times to come.

Finally, good design is definitely seen as

important by the more successful cities. An approach which fosters and encourages the highest achievements in architecture, planning and urban design can help significantly to raise the image of a city, which is important in the process of attracting inward investment. The successes in the USA are clear to see, and in Britain there have been significant achievements, but nothing can compare with the transformation of Barcelona, or the huge scale of the inner-city developments in France, the Netherlands and Germany.

Future generations will judge today's level of civilization and culture in many ways. One will most certainly be related to the legacy of the built environment that is passed on to them. The re-emergence of the inner cities as pleasant places in which to live and work could be one of the greatest achievements of the present day to convey to the next century and beyond. It merely requires creative thinking and responsible commitment by those people with the power to make it happen. It is hoped that some of the ideas in this book will offer some inspiration to those involved.

References

Introduction

1 Falk, N., 'Urban Regeneration', *The Architects' Journal*, 9 December 1992, Volume 196, Number 23, p. 42.

2 Loos, Adolf, from an article by John Olley entitled 'Streets Ahead', *The Architects' Journal*, 30 October 1991, Volume 194, Number 18, pp. 34–37.

Chapter 1

1 Jacobs, J., *Death and Life of Great American Cities*, Jonathan Cape, 1962, pp. 6 and 7.

2 Ibid.

3 Keegan, V., 'The city, centre of recovery', *The Guardian*, (supplement entitled *Olympics 2000*), 6 September 1993, p. 7.

4 Lands, J.D., 'The future of America's central cities', *Built Environment*, Volume 13, Number 4, 1987, pp. 223–241.

5 Dean, A.P., 'The State of the Cities: Paradox', *Architecture*, December 1988, pp. 71–77.

6 Catterill, R., 'The City Killers', *The Guardian*, 30 April 1993.

7 Jacobs, J., p. 200.

8 Ibid., p. 200.

9 Rogers, R., and Fisher, M., *A New London*, Penguin Books, 1992, pp. XV–XVI.

10 Church of England, *Faith in the City, a Call for Action by Church and Nation*, Church House Publishing, 1985, p. 195.

11 Dean, A.O., 'The state of the Cities: Paradox', *Architecture*, December 1988, pp. 71–77.

12 Davy, P., 'Architecture and Housing', *The Architectural Review*, October 1990, Volume CLXXXVIII, Number 1124, p. 35.

13 Ibid.

14 Thornley, A. (editor), *The Crisis in London*, Routledge, 1992, p. 10.

15 Haynes, R., 'Homelessness in the United States', chapter in *Streetwise: Homelessness among the Young in Ireland and Abroad*, edited by Stanislaus Kennedy, The Glendale Press, 1987, pp. 39–46. Also Fodor, T.P. and Grossman, L.S., 'Housing the Homeless: SROs and Transitional Housing: Critical Responses', *Built Environment*, Volume 14, Number 3/4, pp. 209–218.

16 Fenton, N., 'Streetchildren – key issues in the European perspective', chapter in *Streetwise*, pp. 57–64.

17 'Update on Homelessness', *Housing Review*, Volume 42, Number 3, May–June 1993, p. 38.

18 For further information on Foyer housing contact: The Foyer Federation, 91 Brick Lane, London.

19 Department of the Environment, *Action for Cities*, HMSO, London, p. 9.

20 Whitehead, M., *The Health Divide: irregularities in health in the 1980s*, The Health Education Authority, London, 1987, p. 2.

21 Church of England, *Faith in the City*, p. 270.

22 Jacobs, J., pp. 32–33.

23 Scarman, Lord Leslie (Inquiry Report Chairman), *Brixton Disorders*, HMSO, 1981.

24 Church of England, *Faith in the City*, p. 333.

25 Compare this photograph with fig. 2.119, p. 137. *Housing Design in Practice*, Colquhoun, Ian and Fauset, Peter G., Longman UK Ltd, 1991.

26 *The Guardian*, 5 April 1991.

27 Department of Transport/Government Statistical Service (1990). Transport Statistics for London, London, DoT/GSS – information taken from *The Crisis of London*, edited by Andy Thornley.

28 Bushell, C. (editor), *Jane's Urban Transport Systems*, London, Janes Information Group, 1989.

29 'The Architectural Heritage Fund, Annual Reports', obtained from 17 Carlton House Terrace, London SW1Y 5AW also: Bristol Buildings Preservation Trust Ltd, 72–74 Colston Street, Bristol, and, 8–10 West Street, Old Market, Bristol.

30 Petherick, A., and Fraser, R., *Introduction to 'Living over the Shop'*, The University of York, 1992.

31 Department of the Environment, *Sport and Active Recreation Provision in the Inner Cities*, HMSO, 1989, p. 23.

32 For guidance on the level of, and the type of provision, see *Housing Design in Practice*, Colquhoun, Ian and Fauset, Peter G., pp. 222–230.

33 Lewis, P., 'Raising the tone raises the profile', *The Times*, 12 February 1993, p. 39.

34 *The Architects' Journal*, 16 February 1977, Volume 165, Number 7, and Ward, C., pp. 295–298. (Professor Phal originally made the suggestions in his summing up of the 'Save our Cities' Conference, sponsored by the *Sunday Times* and the Gulbenkian Foundation, Bristol 1976.)

35 Liggens, D., *Urban Features*, Volume 1, 1988, p. 10.

36 *The Planner*, 4 September 1992, Volume 78, No. 16, p. 16.

37 MacCormac, R., RIBA President, Forward to the exhibition entitled 'Reviving Cities Urban Design in Action', held at 66 Portland Place, London, between 1–17 June 1993.

38 Aldous, A., *Inner City Regeneration and Good Design*, written for the Royal Fine Arts Commission, pp. 7, 14–17.

39 Ibid., p. 15.

Chapter 2

1 Hall, Professor P., *Cities for Tomorrow*, Basil Blackwell, Oxford and Cambridge (USA), p. 358.

2 Ibid, p. 348.

3 Ibid, p. 358.

4 Campbell, R., 'Shattering Old Housing Myths', article in *Architectural Record*, July 1992, pp. 70–71.

5 Fodor, T.P. and

Grossman, L.S., 'Housing the Homeless: SRO's and Transitional Housing: Critical Responses', article in *Built Environment*, Volume 14, Numbers 3/4, 1988, pp. 209–219.

6 Ibid, p. 215.

7 Barker, P., 'Street violence for export', *The Guardian*, 4 December 1993, p. 25.

8 Levinson, N., 'Rethinking Boston', *Architectural Record*, March 1991, pp. 66 and 67.

9 For further information: Campbell, R., 'Not just another mall', *Architectural Record*, May 1991, pp. 96–103.

10 'Tent City', *Urban Land*, December 1990, p. 22.

11 Cantey, D., 'Baltimore's Lively Downtown Lagoon', *Architecture*, June 1981, p. 33.

12 Ibid., pp. 33–40.

13 Lorenz, C., 'Downtown Lights', *Building Design*, 20 September 1991, No. 1049, pp. 16–18.

14 Ibid, p. 17.

15 Hoyle, B.S., Pinder, D.A. and Husain, M.S. (editors), *Revitalising the Waterfront*, Belhaven Press, London and New York, 1988, p. 156.

16 Usborne, D., 'City on the road back from a high-rise hell', *Independent on Sunday*, 19 December 1993, p. 16.

17 Ibid.

18 For further information: Pearson, C.A., 'Beyond Shelters', *Architectural Record*, July 1992, pp. 84–91.

19 Pearson, C.A., 'After building homeless shelters, a non-profit group builds permanent housing for families', *Architectural Record*, July 1992, pp. 110–112.

20 Ibid.

21 Werth, J., 'Neighborhood Revitalisation: Four Success Stories', *Urban Design International*, 1985, pp. 14–17.

22 Barnett, J., 'Urban Design as a Survival Tool', *Urban Design International*, 1984, pp. 7–40.

23 Interview with housing developers McCormack Baron Associates, September 1992.

24 Leader article, *Architecture*, April 1989, p. 61.

25 Ibid, p. 65.

26 Ibid, p. 66.

27 See: 'The Nation's Largest Single Act of Rehabilitation', *Architecture*, April 1989, pp. 83–85.

28 For further information: 'Union Station', *Urban Land*, December 1991, p. 24. Also 'St Louis Union Station, St Louis, USA', *Architektur + Wettbewerbe* 140/1989, p. 12.

29 Ledewitz, S., 'Pittsburgh: New Houses in Old Neighbourhoods', *Urban Design International*, 1984, p. 37.

30 Freeman, A., 'Fine tuning: A Landmark of Adaptive Use', *Architecture*, November 1986, pp. 67–70.

31 *Architecture*, March 1985, Volume 74, No. 3, pp. 147–148. See also Colquhoun, I. and Fauset, P.G., 'Housing Design in Practice', Longman UK, 1991, p. 136.

32 Linn, C., 'Building Delancy', *Architectural Record*, July 1992, pp. 72–77.

33 Ibid, p. 74.

34 Canty, D., 'Bright and Serene', *Architectural Record*, August 1991, pp. 92–95.

35 Porter, D.R., 'Mission (Almost) Impossible', *Urban Land*, January 1992, pp. 27–31.

Chapter 3

1 Church of England, *Faith in the City: A call for action by Church and Nation*, Church House Publishing, 1987.

2 Coupland, A. 'Docklands: Dream or Disaster': a chapter of *The Crisis of London*, Thornley, A. (editor), Routledge, 1992, p. 155.

3 Ibid., p. 4.

4 Home Office, *Safer Cities Progress Report 1989–90*, HMSO, London, 1990.

5 Stewart, M. 'Ten years of inner cities policy', *Town Planning Review*, Volume 58, Number 2, April 1987.

6 Royal Institute of British Architects, *Inner Cities: the problems and the opportunities*, 1987.

7 Audit Commission, *Urban Regeneration and Economic Development: The Local Government Dimension*, HMSO, 1991, pp. 1–5.

8 Ibid.

9 Ward, C., *Welcome Thinner City*, Bedford Square Press of the National Council for Voluntary Organisations, London, 1989, p. 47.

10 Charles, Prince of Wales, *A Vision of Britain – a personal view of Architecture*, Doubleday, London, 1989.

11 Aldous, A., *Urban Villages*, Urban Villages Group, 1992.

12 Glasgow District Council, 'The East End Experience', 1988, as written in *Glasgow's Glasgow*, published by The Words and the Stones, Glasgow, 1990, p. 185.

13 Donnison, D., and Middleton, A., *Regenerating the City: Glasgow's Experience*, Routledge and Kegan Paul, London, 1987, p. 221.

14 Ibid, pp. 286–291.

15 Cruickshank, D., 'Glasgow Renaissance', *The Architects' Journal*, 27 November 1991, Number 22, Volume 194, pp. 26–30.

16 Pickles, H., 'Going for Growth', *Intercity*, July/August 1992, pp. 42–44.

17 Hetherington, P., 'Church builds on inner-city success story', *The Guardian*, 11 October 1993, p. 20.

18 Couch, D., *Urban Renewal: Theory and Practice*, MacMillan Education Ltd, Basingstoke and London, 1990, pp. 172–4.

19 Ward, C., p. 81.

20 Balls, A., 'Urban Renewal: opportunities and possibilities', *The Planner*, 27 November 1992, Volume 78, Number 21, pp. 16–17.

21 Pivarro, A., 'Sheffield', *Architecture Today*, Number 10, June 1991, pp. 16–19.

22 RIBA, *Reviving Cities, Urban Design in Action*, 1993.

23 Whittaker, M., 'Leeds: has the renaissance come', *Architecture Today*, February 1990, Number 5, pp. 15–16.

24 Osborne, T., 'Swansea: a multi-zone Revitalisation Project', *Built Environment*, Volume 12, Number 3, 1988, pp. 128–137.

25 The Office of Population Census and Surveys, 1984, 1987. The exact figures for population loss from Inner London are: 1961–71, -460,944; 1971–81, -53,957; 1981–86, -8,500. Information from Rogers R. and Fisher, M., *A New London*, Penguin Books, 1992, pp. 30 and 230.

26 Edwards, B., 'Deconstructing the City', *The Planner*, February 1993, Volume 79, Number 2, pp. 16–23.

27 Hall, Professor P., *Cities of Tomorrow*, Basil Blackwell, Oxford, England and Cambridge, Massachusetts, 1988, p. 351.

28 London Docklands Development Corporation (LDDC), *Decade of Achievement*, LDDC, 1991, p. 26.

29 Ibid., p. 26.

30 Brownhill, S., *Developing London's Docklands*, Paul Chapman Publishing Ltd, London, 1990, p. 93.

31 Ibid., p. 70.

32 Ibid., p. 160.

33 Ibid., p. 161.

34 Edwards, Professor B., *London's Docklands*, Butterworth Architecture, 1992, p. 111.

35 Docklands Consultative Committee, *The Docklands Experiment*, p. 19, 1990, from Edwards, B., p. 67.

36 For further information on Compass Point see Colquhoun, I., and Fauset, P.G., *Housing Design in Practice*, Longman UK, 1991, p. 256.

37 Edwards, B., p. 96.

38 Ibid., p. 33.

39 Ibid., p. 99.

40 Ibid., p. 111.

41 Travis, A., 'Docklands fiasco sinks office plans', *The Guardian*, 25 January 1993, p. 20.

42 Vidal, J., 'Thames revival plan wishful thinking', *The Guardian*, 25 March 1993, p. 4.

Chapter 4

1 Rogers, R. and Fisher, M., *A New London*, Penguin Books, 1992, p. 37.

2 Slessor, C., 'A Song for Europe', *The Architectural Review*, January 1993, Volume CXCII, Number 1151, p. 19.

3 Thompson, R., 'Responding to the Challenges of the European Policy and Funding' (paper presented to the RTPI Summer School, 1992), *The Planner*, 27 November 1992, Volume 78, Number 21, pp. 24–26.

4 van Krimpen, A., *Gateway Rotterdam*, The Tree House Publishing Company, 15, Rotterdam, 1990, p. 58.

5 Ibid., p. 58.

6 Ibid., p. 63.

7 Wates, N., 'Netherlands' neighbourhood architects', *The Architects' Journal*, 30 August 1978, Volume 168, Number 35, pp. 374–376.

8 Couch, C., *Urban Renewal – Theory and Practice*, MacMillan Education Ltd, 1990, pp. 109–110.

9 Cruickshank, D., 'Berlin', *The Architects' Journal*, 24 June 1992, Number 25, Volume 195, pp. 20–25.

10 Hall, Professor P., *Cities of Tomorrow*, Basil Blackwell Inc., 1990, pp. 119–121.

11 Clelland, D., 'West Berlin 1984, The Milestone and the Millstone', *The Architectural Review*, September 1984, Volume CLXXVI, Number 1051, pp. 19–22.

12 Ibid., p. 170.

13 Hoffman-Axthelm (1984) Geschichte und Besonderheit der Kreuzberger Mischung, in Senator fur Bau- und Wohnungswesen (ed. 'Kreuzberger Mischung...', op. cit., pp. 9–20, taken from Hass-Klau, Carmen, 'Berlin: "Soft" Urban Renewal in Kreuzberg', *Built Environment*, (edited at the School of Planning Studies, University of Reading), Volume 12, Number 3, Alexandrine Press, pp. 165–175.

14 Davy, P., 'Altbau: Stern Work', *The Architectural Review*, April 1987, Vol. CLXXXI, No. 1082, pp. 87–89.

15 Ibid.

16 Bunting, Madeleine, 'Rebirth of Block 103', *Environment Guardian*, Friday 31 August 1990, p. 21.

17 Davey, P., 'Cologne Integration', *The Architectural Review*, December 1980, Volume CLXVIII, Number 1006, pp. 336–341.

18 Rattenbury, K., 'Booming Tales', *Building Design*, 4 December 1992, Number 1105, p. 18.

19 Welsh, J., 'When the boat comes in', *Building Design*, 9 April 1993, Number 1119, pp. 12–13.

20 *Building Design*, 4 December 1992, Number 1105, p. 18.

21 Venuti, G.C., 'Bologna: From Expansion to Transformation', *Built Environment*, Volume 12, Number 3, 1986, pp. 138–144.

22 Kostof, S., *The City Assembled*, Thames and Hudson, London, 1992, pp. 303–4.

23 'Morphological' I take to mean the study of form and

structure of the individual building.

24 'Topological': pertaining to the study of common historical features found in any group of buildings.

25 'Bologna', *Urban Design Quarterly*, April 1991, p. 12.

26 Cruickshank, D., 'Genoa Drama', *The Architectural Review*, January 1993, Volume CXCII, Number 1151, pp. 36–41.

27 Brookes A. and Stacey M., 'Transit Systems: Genoa', *The Architects' Journal*, 8 April 1992, Volume 195, Number 14, p. 39.

28 Lumley, I., 'Dublin', *The Architects' Journal*, 2 and 9 January 1991, Volume 193, Numbers 1 and 2, pp. 56–57.

29 Slessor, C., 'Dublin Renaissance', *The Architectural Review*, January 1993, Volume CXCII, Number 1151, pp. 42–45.

30 Ibid.

31 Group 91 comprises the following practices: Shay Cleary, Grafton Architects, Paul Keogh, McCullough Mulvin, McGarry Ni Eanaigh, O'Donnell and Tuomey, Shane O'Toole, Derek Tynan.

32 Slessor, C., 'Irish Reels', *The Architectural Review*, January 1993, Volume CXCII, Number 1151, pp. 46–49.

33 Ibid., p. 46.

34 Pater, F.A. 'Shedlands', *The Architectural Review*, May 1990, Volume CLXXXVII, Number 1119, p. 102.

35 Ibid.

36 Ibid.

37 Anderton, F., 'A Tailoring of Two Cities', *The Architectural Review*, May 1990, Volume CLXXXVII, Number 1119, pp. 70–73.

38 Davies, C., 'Carré Culturel', *The Architectural Review*, July 1993, Volume CXCIV, Number 1157, pp. 18–31.

39 'Wohnhaus "Nemausus" in Nîmes, Frankreich', *aw – architektur + wettbewerbe* 136/1988, pp. 18–19.

40 'Catex Factory' and 'Barcelona Activa', *The Architectural Review*, December 1991, Volume CLXXXIX, Number 1138, pp. 26–31 and 44–47.

Bibliography

ALDOUS, ANTHONY, *Inner City Regeneration and Good Design*, Royal Fine Arts Commission, 1992
Urban Villages, Foreword by HRH The Prince of Wales, The Urban Villages Group, 1992

ANDERTON, F., 'Vive la Regional France', *The Architectural Review*, May 1990, Vol. CLXXXVII, No. 1119
'A Tailoring of Two Cities', *The Architectural Review*, May 1990, Vol. CLXXXVII, No. 1119

The Architects' Journal – Special Report 'Housing Refurbishment', 10 February 1993, Vol. 197, No. 6

AUDIT COMMISSION, *The Urban Experience – Observations from Local Value for Money Audits*, Occasional Paper, No. 17, October 1991
Urban Regeneration and Economic Development: The Local Government Dimension, HMSO, London, 1991

BALLS, A., 'Urban Renewal: opportunities and possibilities', *The Planner*, 27 November 1992, Vol. 78, No. 21

BARNETT, J., Urban Design as a Survival Tool', *Urban Quarterly*

BROWNHILL, S., *Developing London's Docklands*, Paul Chapman Publishing Ltd, London, 1990

BUNTING, MADELEINE, 'Rebirth of Block 103', *Environment Guardian*, 31 August 1990

BUTLER, STUART and KONRATAS, ANNA, *Out of the Poverty Trap, A Conservation Strategy for Welfare Reform*, The Free Press, New York, 1987

BUSHELL, C. (Editor), *Jane's Urban Transport Systems, London*, Jane's Information Group.

CAMPBELL, ROBERT, 'Not Just Another Mall', *Architectural Record*, May 1991
Shattering Old Housing Myths, *Architectural Record*, July 1991.

CANTY, DONALD, 'Baltimore's Lively Downtown Lagoon', *Architecture*, June 1981
'Bright and Serene', *Architectural Record*, August 1991

CATTERILL, R., 'The City Killers', *The Guardian*, 30 April 1993

CHARLES, PRINCE OF WALES, *A Vision of Britain – A Personal View of Architecture*, Doubleday, London, 1989

CHURCH OF ENGLAND, *Faith in the City, a Call for Action by Church and Nation*, Church House Publishing, 1985

CLELLAND, D., 'West Berlin 1984, The Milestone and the Millstone', *The Architectural Review*, September 1984

COLQUHOUN, IAN, and FAUSET, PETER G., *Housing Design in Practice*, Longman Scientific and Technical, London, 1991

COMMUNE DI BOLOGNA, *Assessorata alla Programmazione e Assetto Urbano – Rianamento Conservativo del Centro Storico di Bologna*, City Council of Bologna, 1979
Per il Recupero Urbano, City Council of Bologna

COUCH, C., *Urban Renewal – Theory and Practice*, MacMillan Education Ltd, 1990

COUPLAND, A., 'Docklands: Dream or Disaster', in *The Crisis of London*, Thornley, A. (ed.), Routledge, London, 1992.

CRUICKSHANK, D., 'Berlin', *The Architects' Journal*, 24 June 1992
'Glasgow Renaissance', *The Architects' Journal*, 27 November 1991, Vol. 194, No. 22

DAVIES, C., 'Carré Cultural', *The Architectural Review*, July 1993, Vol. CXCIV, No. 1157

DAVY, P., 'Architecture and Housing', *The Architectural Review*, October 1990. Vol. CLXXXVIII, No. 1124
'Altbau: Stern Work', *The Architectural Review*, April 1987, Vol. CLXXXI, No. 1082

'Cologne Integration', *The Architectural Review*, December 1980, Vol. CLXVIII, No. 1006

DEAN, ANDREA O., 'The State of the Cities: Paradox', *Architecture*, December 1980

DEPARTMENT OF THE ENVIRONMENT, *Sport and Active Recreation Provision in the Cities*, HMSO, London, 1989

DONNISON, D., and MIDDLETON, A., *Regenerating the City: Glasgow's Experience*, Routledge and Kegan Paul, London, 1987

EDWARDS, B., 'Deconstructing the City', *The Planner*, February 1993, Vol. 79, No. 2
London Docklands, Butterworth Architecture, London, 1992

ELLIS, C., 'Paris High Street, and Parisian Green', *The Architectural Review*, March 1992, Vol. CXC, No. 1141

FODER, T. P., and GROSSMAN, L. S., 'Housing the Homeless', *Built Environment*, Vol. 14, Numbers 3 and 4, 1988.

FREEMAN, ALLEN, 'The Nation's Largest Single Act of Rehabilitation', *Architecture*, April 1989
'Fine Tuning, A Landmark of Adaptive Use', *Architecture*, November 1986

GLASGOW DISTRICT COUNCIL, 'The East End Experience, 1988', from *Glasgow's Glasgow, The Words and the Stones*, Glasgow, 1990

GRIFFIN, R., 'Persevering in Prague', *The Architects' Journal*.

HALL, D., 'Teeside builds fast track college', *The Architects' Journal*, 7 July 1993, Vol. 198, No. 1.

HALL, PROFESSOR PETER, *Cities of Tomorrow*, Basil Blackwell, Oxford, 1988
'A Partnership for Life', *Building*, 7 July 1978

HOME OFFICE, *Safer Cities Progress Report 1989–90*, HMSO, London, 1990

HILL, S., 'Regenerating a Run-Down Estate', *The Architects' Journal*, 5 May 1993, Vol. 197, No. 18

HOYLE, B. S., PINDER, D. A. and HUSAIN, M. S., (eds), *Revitalising the Waterfront*,

Belhaven Press, London and
New York, 1988

JACOBS, JANE, *Death and Life
of Great American Cities*,
Jonathan Cape, London, 1962

KEATING, M., *The city that
refused to die. Glasgow: the
politics of urban regeneration*,
Aberdeen University Press,
Aberdeen, 1986

KOSTOF, S., *The City
Assembled*, Thames and
Hudson Ltd, London, 1992

LEDEWITZ, STEFANI, 'New
Houses in Old
Neighbourhoods', *Urban Land*,
December 1991

LEWIS, P., 'Raising the Tone
Raises the Profile', *The Times*,
12 February 1993

LEVINSON, NANCY,
'Rethinking Boston',
Architectural Record, March
1991

LIGGINS, DAVID, 'Urban
Regeneration – the Minefield
Factor', *Urban Features*, Vol. 1,
No. 1, 1988

LONDON DOCKLANDS
DEVELOPMENT CORPORATION,
(LDDC), *Decade of
Achievement*, LDDC, 1991

LORENZ, D., 'Downtown
Lights', *Building Design*,
Number 1049, 20 September
1991

LINN, CHARLES, 'Building
Delancy', *Architectural Record*,
July 1992

LUMLEY, I., 'Dublin', *The
Architects' Journal*, 9 January
1991, Vol. 193, No. 2.
'The Netherlands', *The
Architectural Review*, Vol.
CLXXVII, No. 1055.

PARIS PROJETS,
*L Amenagement de L'Est de
Paris*, No. 27, 28, 1987

PATER, F. A. 'Shedlands', *The
Architectural Review*, May 1990,
Vol. CLXXXVII, No. 1119

PEARSON, CLIFFORD A.,
'Beyond Shelters and After
Building Homeless Shelters',

Architectural Record, July 1992

PETHERICK, A. and FRASER,
R., *Living over the Shop*, The
University of York, 1992

PICKLES, H., 'Going for
Growth', *Intercity*, July/August
1992

PIVARRO, A., 'Sheffield',
Architecture Today, No. 19,
June 1991

PLACE DE STALINGRAD IN
PARIS, Frakreich, *aw –
architektur + wettbewerbe*, 114/
1990

PORTER, DOUGLAS R.,
'Mission (Almost) Impossible',
Urban Land, January 1992

RATTENBURY, K., Booming
Tales, *Building Design*, 4
December 1992

RICHARDSON, M., 'Travels
with my Angst', *Building
Design*, 23 April 1993

ROGERS, R., and FISHER, M.,
A New London, Penguin 1992

ROYAL INSTITUTE OF BRITISH
ARCHITECTS, *Inner Cities: the
problems and the opportunities*,
1987

*Reviving Cities, Urban Design
in Action* – booklet to
accompany exhibition at RIBA,
1–17 June 1993

ROTTERDAM CITY COUNCIL,
Rotterdam City Plan, July
1992.

RYAN, R., 'Interiors: Making
room for the movies at Temple
Bar', *The Architects' Journal*,
25 November 1992, Vol. 196,
No. 21

SCARMAN, LORD T., (Inquiry
Report Chairman), *Brixton
Disorders*, April 10–12, 1981,
HMSO, London, November
1981

SLESSOR, C., 'Irish Reels',
The Architectural Review,
January 1993, Vol. CXCII,
No. 1151

'A Song for Europe', *The
Architectural Review*, January
1993, Vol. CXCII, No. 1151

STEWART, M., 'Ten Years of

Inner Cities Policy', *Town
Planning Review*, Vol. 58, No.
2, April 1987

*Temple Bar Lives – Winning
Architectural Framework Plan*,
Temple Bar Properties, 1991

THOMPSON, R., 'Responding
to the Challenges of the
European Policy and Funding',
The Planner, 27 November
1992, Vol. 78, No. 21

THORNLEY, A., *The Crisis in
London*, Routledge, London,
1992

TRAVIS, A., 'Docklands fiasco
sinks office plans', *The
Guardian*, 25 January 1993

TUSA, J., *Prague, the City
where time stood still*, BBC TV
1993, first shown 27 June
1993

VAN VEENENDAAL, H., 'The
Amsterdam Waterfront', *The
Planner*, 13 December 1991

VENUTI, PROFESSOR G. C.,
'Bologna: From Expansion to
Transformation', *Built
Environment*, Vol. 12, No. 3,
1986

VIDAL, J., 'Thames revival
plan wishful thinking', *The
Guardian*, 25 March 1993

WARD, COLIN, *Welcome
Thinner City*, Bedford Square
Press, London, 1989

WATES, N., 'Netherlands'
neighbourhood architects', *The
Architects' Journal*, 30 August,
1978.

WELSH, J., 'When the Boat
Comes In', *Building Design*,
No. 1119, 9 April 1993.

WHITEHEAD, M., *The Health
Divide: Irregularities in Health
in the 1980s*, Health Education
Authority, London, 1987

WHITTAKER, M., 'Leeds: has
the renaissance come?'
Architecture Today, February
1990, No. 5

WILSON, J. B., 'The Future
City: Where is the City
Going?' *The Planner*,
25 January 1991

Index